LISTENING TO
COUNTRY

Aboriginal people are respectfully asked to note
that names and photographs of deceased
persons occur in this book.

LISTENING TO COUNTRY

A journey to the heart of what it
means to belong

Ros Moriarty

ALLEN&UNWIN

First published in 2010

Australian Government

This project has been assisted by the Australian Government through the Australia Council for the Arts, its arts funding and advisory body.

Allen & Unwin
83 Alexander Street
Crows Nest NSW 2065
Australia
Phone: (61 2) 8425 0100
Fax: (61 2) 9906 2218
Email: info@allenandunwin.com
Web: www.allenandunwin.com

Cataloguing-in-Publication details are available
from the National Library of Australia
www.librariesaustralia.nla.gov.au

ISBN 978 1 74175 380 6

Set in 12/16 pt Fairfield/Sabon by Midland Typesetters, Australia
Printed and bound in Australia by Griffin Press

10 9 8 7 6 5 4 3 2

To the memory of four strong Australian women: my mother, Nancy Ridley Langham, and my Borroloola mothers-in-law Kathleen O'Keefe Murrmayibinya and Annie Isaac Karrakayn and sister Thelma Douglas Walwalmara

Contents

Prologue

THE IMAGE IS VIVID in my mind. The night I am thinking about is
a clear and recurring memory. Five or six of us are seated on the
ground around a smouldering campfire under a star-filled black
sky by the waters of the Gulf of Carpentaria in Australia's remote
north. It is 1982—twenty-seven years ago. Our baby is sleeping
in a cot nearby. There is no wind, no temperature to notice,
no sounds. The darkness begins immediately behind us. My
husband's uncle, Musso, the ceremonial leader of the Yanyuwa
people, is telling stories about spirit ancestors in the bush
around us, about people leaving their bodies to travel vast
distances, about messages birds and animals bring to people in
danger. Afterwards we drift off to sleep in the total silence.

This same man hauls an enormous sack of writhing crabs
across the mudflats the next day to throw on the coals of the fire.
We share the sweet white flesh with his family. Laughing, talking,
enjoying each other's company. And this same man commands
the hunting boat for dugong, singing the song of the animal's spirit
when it is speared, cutting its portions for distribution according to ritual and protocol. I pick up just a crude inkling of the
interconnection between his powerful culture and the everyday

1

balance of a satisfying life lived in harmony with the elements. In his words and when he is quiet, I sense the sharp wisdom and deep humanity that lies beneath his humility.

We were visiting my husband John's Aboriginal community at Borroloola, in Australia's Northern Territory. It was the start of an extraordinary journey. Not so much because of the terrain or the vistas—as spectacularly different as they were—but because the cultural landscape of family and humanity radiated a warmth that seemed to rise from the baked land itself. In my early twenties, with a baby in tow, the impressions seared into the heart and mind of a white girl from down south were indelible. They were then etched deeper with every trip back over the years, as my own life story became entwined with theirs.

Culture separated the sexes much of the time, and it was the women who showed me a view of the world fundamentally different from any other I knew. Despite their abject material poverty, illness, and the increasing violence in their community, happiness and optimism permeated their lives. The spirit of their men shone too, but I knew custom would dictate that if I could tell anyone's story, it would be mostly that of the women. I knew it wasn't a story I could hurry in the telling. In fact, a quarter of a century of pilgrimages north would go by before I would begin to think seriously about what to tell. And why to tell it.

What to tell would be something of the spiritual wealth that wraps these women tightly together, and which has taught them the rules for happy lives. It would be a story, too, of Australia's identity and its future in the face of the catastrophic legacy colonial collision continues to inflict on Aboriginal people. Why to tell it would be to open a window to the times of Yanyuwa Law women. To reveal a glimpse of the philosophy they have gleaned along humanity's pathway of more than forty thousand years, set

2

down by the oldest living culture on Earth. I felt that in this story others would find moments of inspiration and revelation along their own life journeys, as I had.

We took our children back as babies to the nurturing of the tribe. Old Tim Rakuwurlma, after whom we named our first baby, and who remembered life in the bush well before white men came, announced our little boy's name would be 'Baniyan, cheeky brown snake'. He sang the Baniyan songs which our baby would belong to, and the women cuddled and carried Tim from place to place. Our baby's grandmother, blind from glaucoma, pointed out the night sky constellations that lived in her memory, and sang songs of her Dreamings from those stars. We slept soundly on the ground with the clan group by the campfire, and feasted on fish grilled in the ashes.

Our second son, James, was given the name dugong—Jawarrawarral. Just as Tim would show himself to have a darting imaginative mind as he grew, like a brown snake striking, James would have the deep stillness of his gentle ocean namesake. They were just babies when the old people held them close and named them, giving them their birthright.

When they were a little older, the boys clambered noisily over stones and logs, shinnying up trees, leaping into cascading river pools with local kids. They poked at the eyes of bush turkeys their father shot for dinner, heroes in their school classes for the letters sent home. They urged their uncle Samuel to drive the tin dinghy ever closer to killer crocs sunning themselves on the river's edge, squealing when he turned suddenly, laughing, sending a spray of wake from the boat across the massive scaly animal as it slid into the water under the boat.

Our daughter Julia, born five years after James, was named Marrayalu, the mermaid. Her songs begin near Alice Springs, a thousand kilometres down through the centre of Australia. A rocky outcrop by Wigleys Waterhole spills a seam of glassy quartz down its rounded form. It is the breast milk of the mermaid. The story of mermaid spirits who left the sea to dwell in fresh waterholes starts at this landform, in the middle of Australia's red desert. Julia basked in the stories and in the love of her aunties and grandmothers. She would tag along behind the line of women collecting sugarbag (bush honey) from craggy tree trunks, sucking at the gluey sweetness of the chunks they gave her.

The children's Borroloola world was a universe away from our usual life in the city. Spotlighting the eyes of crocs at night along the riverbank, eating dugong meat boiled up on the fire, tearing around the Gulf in a boat hunting turtle. They would float on their backs in wonder on a steaming thermal lake under soaring red cliffs, and paddle a boat through canopies of foliage draped with tree snakes.

But the spiritual difference went deeper than the physical, and it began to emerge in layers, a little more every time we went back. During the quiet times of sitting down by the riverbank with family in the morning, cooking by the fire at night, in the boat drifting around at the creek mouth in search of fish. It was of course natural to John, in his pores and under his skin, but to me it was a gradual revelation. The intellectual complexity of it, disguised by understatement, offered veiled viewing. Travelling with small children in the oppressive climate, and my impatience with a slower, foreign world, restricted my senses in the beginning. While freely given, it would take time for me to feel the arms of inclusion.

John continued the children's teaching back home. Even in the city he pointed out the cleverest of camouflaged insects, identified birdcalls in the street, and drew animal tracks on the sand at the beach. He taught them the silence of listening out of doors, and shared the taste of bush berries and fruits on walks into the scrub. The stories he told them were bedtime favourites, and kept them connected to their Yanyuwa family.

Borroloola family visited us in Adelaide, often travelling by air for the first time. John's stepfather, Willie, had never seen a washing machine before, describing to Kathleen, John's mother, the vortex of water that rushed all by itself, in and out of the clothes. Kathleen ended up in John's arms when a lion roared at Adelaide Zoo. Uncles and cousins came with us to France and Japan, touching the stone of Notre Dame—'proper old, this place, eh'—and asking John if there were crocodiles in the Seine. They smiled shyly at the attention from leggy French girls when they jammed on didgeridoo in Parisian bars. They declared sushi in Tokyo to be just like the bait they ate when the fish weren't biting. The constellations of the Northern Hemisphere night sky were baffling, and the mystery of the time difference was the focus of most phone calls home.

We visited Borroloola as often as we could put jobs on hold, jump in the car and head three thousand kilometres north. With each visit, John's mother's generation grew older and physically weaker as the community structures disintegrated around them. Bush food was being hunted out by tourists, dugong and turtle were drowning in the nets of commercial fishermen. Shops stocked the salt- and sugar-laden tinned precursors to heart disease and diabetes. The joy of seeing family was all too often tinged with the sadness of funerals.

When John's mother passed away, we drove back to the Gulf from Tathra on the New South Wales coast where we'd been camping. The children sat cramped and quiet in the car on the road in from Mount Isa, a simple sheaf of long-stemmed white carnations balanced on ice between their seats in the hot, steamy weather. They sweltered in the sticky Wet season heat at the bush cemetery, joining the grieving line to scatter red sand gently onto their Abuji's tiny coffin. John's mother took with her fluency in eight Aboriginal languages, and the complete and sophisticated knowledge of a senior Law woman. She took with her secrets that the sacred Law forbade her to pass on to those who had not been ceremonially prepared to receive them. I sensed both her frustration and acquiescence in the silence the Law demanded of her to erase the irreplaceable.

Yet despite the loss and the deprivations, the same as Indigenous communities the world over, a deep sense of the spirit has not deserted the older women of my husband's family. The rich warmth of their human connection has endured. It seems to be a connection that goes further than most of us experience in our developed-world relationships, where we hurry through the competitive ambitions that drive us. Over the years of visits back to Borroloola, I've seen how these women are able to give and receive happiness in the face of chronic disadvantage. I have wondered if it springs from the nourishing spirituality that envelops them, if it is embedded in the continuation of culture, in the retention of language that interprets their world. In the comfort of the rules and traditions that family has carefully set down for them. I wonder if we have traded enduring happiness in the first world by our increasing rejection of things spiritual, esoteric and ancestral.

It seems there is a pathway gouged by a metaphorical river of intricate knowledge and wisdom deep inside my husband's community, which feeds a positive outlook in the face of dire hardship. It is clear that people's lives are not without sadness, but they find a way to nurture the spirit. The Yanyuwa call it *anyngkarrinjarra ki-awarawu*, 'listening to country'. It is a time and place to sit down, absorb, reflect, see how things really are in the place you come from. A place in the mind, a place with family, or a physical place where the mind is freed.

In May 2006, I had an unexpected chance to 'listen to country' with the women of my Borroloola family. It is ultimately not just a women's thing, because the culture that demands 'listening to country' weaves its structure around all. But men's business is not for women to describe, and it was the powerful matriarchs of John's tribe who generously took me on an inspiring and humbling journey into their spiritual world. It was an ordinary journey of everyday intimacy with the natural order of life. A simple chance to be still. To 'listen in order to see'. It was a time to begin to tell the story I had wanted to share for so long. A story of a disappearing world hidden behind stigma and prejudice, where family is paramount, nature sustains the spirit, and relationships are enshrined in clear-cut rules. Of contemporary women with old spirits, who have survived a turbulent and violent history of European contact. Who live their difficult lives in a way that brings the happiness of heartful human connection.

In opening a tiny window to their story of 'listening to country', my intent is to honour their wisdom and hear their voices. It is not to use their resilience to excuse the deplorable physical conditions they live in, the result of colonial dispossession and confused, 'out of sight, out of mind' government policies since. Neither is it to pass judgement on the social dysfunction which has decimated their children's generation, forcing these ageing women to bring up their grandchildren. Most of all, it is not to tell their secret, sacred stories. It is to hear their songs, to celebrate their heart and generosity, and to share a glimpse of the philosophical insights which allow them to live their lives with power and meaning. It is to ponder, too, the quiet passing of this last line of full Aboriginal Law women. When our fragile and beautiful land, Australia, will no longer be sung by its first people, and will no longer remember their nurturing, resilient hands.

1

Purpose

anyngkarrinjarra ki-awarawu
Listening in a quiet place lets me see.

When I am still, and the quiet washes over my spirit,
then I can hear. When I find a calm place in my mind,
I can see where to go.

Day 1, Friday 26 May 2006

*t*he Wet was late ending in the Territory this year, but the Dry has arrived now, crisp and clear. We fly in on a skinny prop jet, a pencil with wings, in the middle of the afternoon. Jim Beam and cola is the in-flight beverage of choice for the handful of silver, lead and zinc miners who are returning to work. The airstrip is at Xstrata's McArthur River Mine, slightly under two hours south-east of Darwin on northern Australia's remote Gulf of Carpentaria.

An hour's drive from there is our destination, Borroloola —a far-flung, mostly forgotten outpost in Australia's far north. A 1983 Australian government report describes it as the second-most remote community on the continent, beaten to the honour only by a few households on Western Australia's desiccated Nullarbor Plain. It's the birthplace of my husband John. His Irish father gave him skin that was paler than his tribal Aboriginal mother's, and at four years of age John was stolen. Taken away on the back of an army truck by the welfare and the church to turn him into a white boy three thousand kilometers south in Sydney's Blue Mountains. He remembers that on a rough patch of road during the journey a wooden box shifted and fell on him, crushing his toe. He remembers crying and crying among floral skirts milling around him.

When I met John's mother, Kathleen Murrmayibinya, in 1978, she was blind from glaucoma, but she showed me where John was born on the riverbank. She told me quietly how one day she took her son to school, and when she went to pick

11

him up he was gone. John's stepfather, Willie Mawurrinji, told us that Kathleen never stopped crying. She was eighteen when John was born, and she didn't give birth again.

John considers himself luckier than most of the 'stolen generation' kids. Surviving a decade of deprivation and abuse in Sydney and Adelaide, he found his mother again when he was fifteen, eleven years and a child's lifetime after he was taken away. He started a journey of reconnection with his family and his Yanyuwa culture. Our regular pilgrimages back to the tribe with our three children since the early 1980s have been part of all our journeys. Seeing Tim Baniyan, James Jawarrawarral and Julia Marrayalu given their names, and nurtured in the community, has been part of the healing— for John's anger and sadness at being taken away; for me as a white Australian witnessing the lifelong pain of such an abhorrent racist government policy in my own country. For the children, it has been about being comfortable in their own skin, in their identity. They are all deeply attached to Borroloola and to John's family.

The memories return today as we fly across the savannah landscape, and brace for a steep, noisy descent. Tears are always near the surface when I see the land that John was ripped away from. In my mind's eye is a rare childhood photo we have of John as a cherubic piccaninny in his grandfather's dugout canoe. Taken in the early 1940s by Merle Griffin, the first white woman to journey by mail truck into the Gulf, the photo found its way to John through a series of coincidences that began with a chance meeting on a Greek ship he sailed to England on in 1962. A fellow passenger was a friend of Merle, and connected traveller John from Borroloola with toddler John from Merle's descriptions. With characteristic optimism, John cites this as one of a string of fortunate things that have happened in his life.

Tim, who will soon be twenty-five, has joined us on this visit. He has come to talk to the men about his stories, for an animated feature film he is working on. I have come to finally start work on a book. James, twenty-two now, has stayed in Sydney to prepare for university exams, and seventeen-year-old Julia is coming to the end of two years' training at a tennis academy in Barcelona, Spain.

After Sydney's late autumn chill, the northern heat wraps around us as we step out onto the tarmac. An insistent, permeating sun, rather than a burning grill. The earth is red, and the shrubby vegetation is one of stripy tones rather than a blanket green. Silvery eucalypt, light, mid and dark greens, yellowy lime, straw-like grasses tinged with burnt sienna. Trees are dotted across escarpment-lined plains, throwing dappled shade. The sky is a clear blue, intense overhead, a little softer on the horizon.

We drive into Borroloola, past humped grey Brahman cattle grazing in the scrub. John points out, as he always does, Frog Dreaming, a huge frog-like rocky outcrop that sits on its own amid trees on the plain, looking back along the Carpentaria Highway. A massive wedge-tailed eagle flies beside us, a piece of hapless prey hanging from its talons. A flock of black cockatoos with a shock of orange tail feathers rises in chorus from the roadside. A pair of brolgas struts near a waterhole still full from the Wet. They are as tall as men. The Gulf is a raw and heady place of rough-hewn beauty.

The Yanyuwa town camp is familiar as we drive in. Mostly dirt track, the small amount of path-sized bitumen road is potholed and dilapidated. The army is putting up a few new houses, but corrugated-iron shanties are home to scores of families in overcrowded and unsanitary conditions. Sickness is rife, and crime and violence are fuelled by alcohol and, increasingly, drugs. As we pull up, tiny kids are playing with sticks among discarded junk. Older kids mill around a blaring sound system pounding out rap. Their parents sit dozing or playing cards near clapped-out car wrecks and empty beer cans.

We find John's tribal sister, Thelma Douglas Walwalmara, first. She is just back from kidney treatment in Darwin. Renal failure is endemic here. Thelma looks older, frail. Long embracing hugs for John and for me. She holds on to Tim, all six feet of him—can't believe how big he has grown. '*Abuji, Abuji*,' grandson, grandson, she croons as she holds him close. Annie Isaac Karrakayn, one of John's tribal mothers, strolls out of her house nearby. More laughter, hugs. She too croons over all of us. John asks how everyone is. 'Too much grog,' Annie tells us. 'No good.'

I feel the usual welling warmth of their embrace of John, of Tim and of me, a love that wraps around us like a mellow spreading thing. Each time we return, the joy of it always takes me a little bit by surprise. This broad extended family tucks its inclusion tightly around us. They tell us 'I love you', 'I miss you', 'Too long since we see you, my son, my daughter-in-law, my grandson'. They give completely from deep inside. Unaffected, no conditions, no question. Not many words are needed. The first time I came I knew I was transparent to them, from the inside out. What I feel, what I think, if I am how I say I am. I know they make allowances for me, excuse me of things. Insensitivities, impatience.

John and I sit down on plastic chairs on the cement slab at the side of Thelma's house. Thelma shoos hairless camp dogs away, others twitch in their sleep on the red dirt. A small boy surrenders his seat for Tim. There is more giggling among us at the pleasure of being together. Then complaints that the men have let the culture go. John explains I have come to do some work on the book I have been talking to them about for a while. About how Borroloola women have a different way of seeing the world. That theirs is the world's oldest culture, and that they carry wisdom handed down through their ancestors for tens of thousands of years. But their world is vanishing. They are the last of their line to have full knowledge, since most of the young women have let the stories go. Annie and Thelma nod, talk about the sadness of losing culture.

We talk of the big issues people need to hear about. 'Like love,' I tell them. 'What you believe about love. What it means.'

'It's when you give something to someone,' Thelma says. Her shabby, overcrowded house is the backdrop to her simple, heartfelt statement.

I feel torn, like I always do in Borroloola. The poverty is stark, confronting. The urge is to fix it, change it, stir things up. Yet I worry that in this urge is my judgement of the reality of their lives. That I am comparing the grind of their very survival with the privileged pleasures of my city-slick comforts. I wonder if my way is really a better way. Or am I ignoring without shame what I would never accept for myself? A few groceries, some tins of Log Cabin tobacco, a little cash, a meal or two at the pub. Time to talk and laugh. These are the things we can bring for family that don't demean the dignity of heartful lives being led. They seem a paltry exchange for the riches of spirit they willingly give us.

It turns out the women can't sit down and talk with me this week. They have to go for ceremony in Kalkaringi, Annie explains. Women's ceremony. 'The Rules, the Business,' Annie says.

John asks if they can delay a few days.

No. They are sorry, but they don't have any choice. It's the Law.

John asks if they will take me with them.

'Yes, Yuwani [daughter-in-law],' Thelma says. 'You can come with us.'

I explain that I have to be back in Borroloola Wednesday to catch the flight out, and ask if that's okay.

Annie, the ceremony boss, says it's not. If I return to my husband before the ceremonies are properly over, he will get sick. They have to finish the ceremonies, then make the whole place clear again, before they can safely leave. Friday is possible, but not Wednesday.

Eight days away. No outside contact. What about my staff, my clients? My life is a gridlocked map of minutes and hours that spin around each other in varying degrees of chaos. The plan was to chat for a couple of days by the river. This is unexpected. Will I be intruding on the ceremony week? The privilege of the invitation is sobering. They've talked about it before. About teaching me to dance. I've just never been in town when the opportunity has come up. I start to do some quick planning. I tell Annie and Thelma I will try to find a car, and we can drive together if they decide they want me to come. I have no idea where Kalkaringi is. Later, when I look at a map, I see that it is in very isolated country, at least ten hours' drive away, maybe more, depending on the passability of roads after the Wet. But I know there will not be too many more chances to make a start on the book. Both Annie and Thelma are ageing quickly. Annie tells me who has authority to talk in the book. Thelma, Dinah, Jemima, Violet, Rosie, Maureen, Thelma Dixon. The senior Law women.

I find a car. It's in the interest of McArthur River Mine's public relations agenda to support local people in maintaining their culture. With the capacity to produce three per cent of the world's zinc, MRM's underground operation is going open cut, with a controversial diversion of the river. They will lend me a diesel Toyota. The conservation lobby and land council have cultivated opposition to the mine in Borroloola. The reality, though, is that without the mine the town would be dead, its population even more reliant on government handouts and the continuing personal indignity of dependence. The best people can hope for is an equitable share of the economic, social and cultural returns that miners must deliver. But it is a difficult, perhaps impossible negotiation for Borroloola people. A complicated and fraught history dating back to expansion of the pastoral industry in the Gulf culminated in the mid-1970s, when the Federal government changed foreign investment legislation to allow the miners to buy McArthur River Station and Bing Bong Station over the top of prospective Aboriginal landowners. It was a strategic and convenient purchase, as the mine sat on McArthur River, and Bing Bong became the site of the port for shipping the ore. Having lost access to what was originally Aboriginal land, the only bargaining chip that remains with local people is the paper tiger of moral and political persuasion.

But the bush life has gone, and the cash economy can't be

repealed. Without the mine, the airport and freight services would close. There is a long way to go in relations between the mine and the community, but it's the mine that has joined the government to talk about building the town's first swimming pool, and its first gym. They are decades overdue in a community where kids are often in detention by their mid-teens. The mine has said it will pay for staff to motivate kids to use the facilities. But in the way of so much in the bush, it is still mostly talk. Yanyuwa women, though, desperately want to divert their grandchildren from the destructive town camp lifestyle that is the only role model they know, and some young Aboriginal men are taking up apprenticeships. The women are more than happy to accept the mine's offer of the car.

The vehicle is a heavy-duty four-wheel drive with a bullbar, two oversized spare tyres, a twenty-litre water container, dual long-distance fuel tanks, and a map extending south-west to the edge of the Tanami Desert, where we are headed. I have never before driven into the outback without John. I don't know how to open the car bonnet or check the oil and water. I get a quick lesson in engaging all-wheel drive. A run-through of the tool kit and how to dislodge the spare tyre chained under the rear if I have a blow-out. A lot of theory.

I pack a few clothes in a bag, grab a torch, an aluminium mug, fork, knife and spoon, and my swag to sleep in. My swag is one of the favourite things I own. It's a canvas bag of about my height, with a mattress, sleeping quilt and pillow inside. It has insect netting at the opening, and rolls up and clips with straps for easy transport. Just seeing it sitting in the shed always evokes the peace of starlit sleeping. I'd brought it with me in the expectation we might spend a night or two out bush. It would now be put to much greater use.

Tim manages to log into satellite internet in this town where, in twenty-first-century Australia, our mobile phones are useless. I scribble emails to staff and clients, signing out for the next eight days. I email Julia to tell her what I'm doing, and wish her luck in a tournament about to start in Madrid. I already feel sick in the stomach at the thought of missing my daily phone calls to her. It is the only way I cope with her being so far away while so young. I email James in Sydney asking him to ring her, and to keep in touch with his father through Tim's satellite email. I get an early night ahead of a long drive west.

I MET JOHN WHEN I was a twenty-one-year-old researcher at the Department of Aboriginal Affairs in Canberra. He was thirty-nine. On my first day there, one of the secretaries told me that John Moriarty was perfectly at home in the Prime Minister's office, but knew the real bush stuff, too. It turned out to be true, although I didn't think about it much at the time—I was too busy falling in love with him. He was very good-looking, funny and sensitive. Our romance was not politically smart for a senior black public servant—I was too young and too white. But the caustic gossip evaporated in the steam of the passion between us.

Ours was hardly an orthodox courtship. The first time I met John's mother, Kathleen, we ate succulent, smoky freshwater turtle—straight from the fire where she had cooked it. As an initiation, I was glad it wasn't the snake or goanna of John's child-hood. The turtle limbs were delicious, a little like the moist bony bits of chicken. I could see why it was prized tucker. The home Kathleen shared with John's stepfather was a rusting car trailer in the scrub. The elevated base of the trailer gave them protection from stampeding buffalo and snakes. The tarp draped over the top kept out the chill of Dry season nights, but wasn't much use against the torrential rains and cyclonic winds of the summer Wet. In one rampaging storm, Willie and Kathleen somehow survived by lying under a wrecked car.

Kathleen had the most finely sculpted hands I had ever seen. They were a lot like John's. She told me about John being taken away when he was a little fella. They told her he was going to school for the day. They didn't bring him back. Kathleen didn't see him, or know where he was, for ten years. Her helplessness made me feel dizzy.

Kathleen told me about the riverbank where John was born; ''im born old bush way,' she chuckled. She pointed to the place over her shoulder with her lips. The same signal John gives me when he lip points to the door to leave a party or a dinner. She smiled and cried in the telling of her only baby's birth.

John says he counts his blessings that he found his mother again. During a church holiday to Alice Springs when he was fifteen, a slight, dignified Aboriginal woman walked across the street to ask him his name. 'John Moriarty,' he told her. She replied, 'I'm your mother.' They just sat down by the side of the road on the ground, and touched hands. 'I am sorry, my son, your grandmother's gone,' were her first words. 'Why did you let me go?' were John's. It was the start of his journey home. Not right away, because the Protector of Aborigines sent Kathleen back north, and John back south. But John finally knew there was a place where he would belong.

In those years of belonging to come, they would never talk much about the time he was gone. Torn away from a loving family in a land of plenty, the pain of the childhood her boy had missed was too great for Kathleen, and the world John entered down south held agonies he would never want his mother to know.

His abduction was in line with a bizarre government policy that aimed to 'smooth the dying pillow' of 'full blood' Aborigines, by stamping out the Aboriginality of young, paler children. Lessons in how to hold a teacup and the art of scrubbing floors were dished out alongside hunger and abuse. School was a barefoot walk away in the frost, orange peels and gum from tree trunks filled up some of the gnawing holes in their stomachs, and sermons told them they would be washed as white as snow in the blood of the Lamb. Paler, of course, is not in any sense an absolute, and there wasn't any sort of blood that would make their blackness white. For that, John has always been extremely grateful.

John's story came out in the quiet times when we talked. When we threw some chops in a pan by highland lakes around Canberra, and slept under the moon. When he chiselled a spear and honed it over a fire in the scrub. Or brought honey ants from the desert to the office, and taught me to bite the sugary sac on their backs. When he sat strumming a few chords on a guitar and sang a verse or two of a country song, I realised the miracle was not just what he'd survived: it was the spirit of his survival. Something in him had decided early, long before a child should know about such decisions, that nothing would break him. Not the beatings with a rubber hose when he was naked and wet from a shower; not digging a baby's grave when he was just a small child himself; not the crying for his nine-year-old friend whose mother died, even though he was the same age and had no idea where his own mother was. Somewhere deep inside, he tucked away the hope of Borroloola's love.

The parched land of the Northern Territory embodied a lot of longing for John. Its power ran deeper than his memory. It took time for me to understand. To acquire a taste for its bony red ochres and powdery brown charcoals. Even its filmy greens and languid blues in the Wet were at first unsatisfying to my mind's eye, trapped in the lushness of a Tasmanian childhood. In the bush of our holidays in the far reaches of the wild west coast's Pieman River, where perennial rain and ancient huon pines of the Tarkine blended together in primordial vistas. Or on breathy climbs to the summits of Cradle Mountain, Mount Roland and Mount Olympus, where the air was brittle like ice. The lakes inked with translucent indigo. And the silence so loud it intoxicated.

Until I moved to university in Canberra, I'd thought I'd grown up in the city. But seaside Devonport was just a cosy country town back then, the pace of life swelling only a little with the waves from Bass Strait that carried the *Princess of Tasmania* ferry from Melbourne to her mooring twice a week. Artists, musicians and people who loved the bush loved living in Tasmania. We were all of those. My mother's mother Ruby was a fine painter in oils. My mother's sister Lully, a contralto, was in demand for the Repertory Society's musicals all along the coast. Ma, my father's mother, and his sister, Aunty Rose, crocheted intricate webs of linen and lace.

My childhood school nights were a flurry of preludes and fugues, escalating as Monday's piano lesson with Mrs Herbert drew near. Weekends were as often as not taken up with performing at Uncle Vernon's concert parties in Devonport's hilly hinterland, the luscious country cakes and steaming thermoses reward enough for singing, playing and acting the night away at local church halls. 'Mammy's Little Baby' was a song I rendered with full voice and charcoal-blackened face, as I crooned to my 'Black Sal' doll, my hair tied up in a red and white spotted headscarf to match hers. Our finale was often calypso, all grass skirts swishing and tan cream melting in the footlights.

Boats and fish and tents on the sand followed noisy family Christmases on trestle tables under rose-clad lattice. My father taught us to love the sea off the bluff, bobbing around for the rock cod to bite; the streams in the mountains where dye from the trees threw clear brown shadows into rock pools; and the enticing but dangerous waters of Bass Strait, which lured him to many a foolhardy crossing.

Life was Methodist and modest. Enough on the table, never to waste. Life was enduringly familiar, and the few immigrants in our town didn't seem very foreign. The Dutch families with their piggeries a bus ride from school, their gift shops in town, and hard-working children in class. The Scotsmen who wore berets to church, and the English who taught their gardens to bloom.

It was a quiet and gentle way to spend a childhood, and its shackles were easily severed by many of the island's youth, like me, making their post-school exodus to bigger ponds. My intense fondness for this place's warmth and generosity grew only with the decades of distance. It was later, too, that I realised the influence of Tasmania's seductive physicality in my life. Of the way landscape shapes the senses.

The Tassie I grew up in had not changed at all by the time I arrived back at twenty-three, with my intended Aboriginal husband in tow. Cousins were marrying their childhood sweethearts, and school friends each other. If it fazed anyone that I was marrying a black man instead, they had the good manners not to show it. Some older aunts viewed us with a twinkle in their eye. It wasn't John's first visit. In twists of fate that have marked so much of John's life, he'd travelled the length and breadth of the island in 1960, photographing a house in historic Deloraine which turned out to be my grandmother's, and walking the mountains with Franz Ezelboch, a naturalist hermit who had held me as a small child in a picture at Cradle National Park the same year John walked with him.

Borroloola could have been another planet. I'd not knowingly met a single Aboriginal person growing up. School courses had airbrushed our history, told us that in the 1850s the penal colony of Tasmania had acted for the good of the remaining descendants of the 'Tasmanoids', relocating them to the rugged, windswept islands of the Bass Strait. In fact it had been genocide, luring people into entrapment with rations and clothes. Those who'd escaped the net had remained in various pockets of the state— including, as I discovered later, dusky-skinned cousins on my father's side. My father's sister told me stories too, of the 'black blood' in my mother's family from up behind Mole Creek, but any such heritage remains romantically shrouded in tasty genealogies of convicts, Welsh clergy and publicans.

Singing and piano at Melbourne University's Conservatorium of Music had loomed as the preparation for my likely career, but the concert stage was not to be. A mix-up in enrolments took me instead to the Australian National University in Canberra to prepare for a career teaching Japanese back in Tasmania. The prospect of teaching dimmed, the degree turned into French and linguistics, and my life became permanently moored to the mainland. Canberra became a longer term prospect following university and, after a few holiday jobs, Aboriginal Affairs was the place where I began a life's work. It was where something of my destiny would unwind.

The Australia I found as a young government researcher was often remote and foreign. When I was just twenty-one, two Arrente women, Cathy Abbott and Marilyn Armstrong, drove me through the Central Australian desert from Alice Springs to their home community in Hermannsburg. I had been dispatched from Canberra to talk to the leaders of the family outstations dotted along the ridges and dry creek beds of this crusty country, to see how government services were working. Just after we arrived at dusk, the men drove in with a recently killed 'roo in the back of their sand-coated ute. It was dark by the time the whole carcass was thrown on the fire. It was impossible to see much of the meat we ate in the firelight, but it was not an offensive taste. I could tell by its texture that it was seared rather than cooked.

My 'bedroom' at the Wallace Rock Hole outstation was a tiny corrugated-iron cubicle, with just a wire bed and mattress. It was freezing in the desert night, and unbearably hot in the day. The only English I heard spoken that week was a few translated answers to my questions. There was little I found that resembled my experience of the country I'd been born in. I looked uncomfortably for cues of inclusion, and swallowed the loneliness of cold, silent nights in my tiny hut. People were not unwelcoming. They were just going about lives which were unfamiliar to me. I quickly understood how alienating such an experience of dislocation from culture could be. For me, being an outsider was a few weeks out of my year. For many of the Aboriginal people I was meeting, it was most of the years out of their lives.

Moved indiscriminately from their traditional lands and herded together in the Hermannsburg Lutheran mission, life and the authorities had handed these people a rough deal. With families becoming tired of the control of the church and the welfare, outstations were a swing in government policy to right the wrongs of dispossession, and the inevitable social fallout of illiteracy and poverty. In effect, people were endeavouring to go back out to the lands they'd been herded in from. Some of the tiny outrider camps were able to secure teachers and health workers on a fairly regular basis. Some were able to keep their youth from drifting into delinquency and detention. Most lived in conditions more usual in Australia's third-world neighbours.

A few months later I took more questions and an aluminium dinghy across the length and breadth of the Torres Strait at Australia's northernmost tip. Don Mosby, a warm and engaging elderly Islander with the thickest spectacles I had ever seen and a squint to match, sat at the bow of the tiny boat, spotting reefs. At the speed we were rocketing across the blue-green waters of the Strait, we definitely would have hit something well before Don saw it. It was a carefree, if precarious, way to travel. I heard stories of families drifting for days in dinghies with broken-down outboards, or which had run out of fuel; most turned up safe and sound eventually, far from their intended destinations.

As we left the mainland for Thursday Island we chugged past Horn Island, where my father had been stationed as an air force electrician in the Second World War. As the sun beat down on my shoulders, and the soupy wind blew hot through my hair, I imagined how foreign it would have been for him here in the tropics. He was an islander too—born on King Island off the north-west coast of Tasmania. But King was as different from Horn as islands could be. Lashed by the freezing seas and gale-force winds of Bass Strait, King Island's fight was with the elements. Horn's was with the Japanese.

Like most of the men and women from the war, my father told little of what he'd seen. As a child, I'd skipped along the edge of Anzac Day marches on Devonport's blustery river shore, where Dad's medals glinted on sunny days. On grey days, when the icy wind bit my ears and toes at the cenotaph, I'd felt even sadder for Sheryl and her sister from my school who led their blind father in the parade.

In the dinghy scooting past Horn, I remembered the look on Dad's face when I asked him about the glory the troops fought to bring to their country. Never, ever, think there's glory in war, he told me. And the finality with which he said it finished the conversation and the matter. In another place, in another time, in the small boat in the Strait, I listened to what was wrapped away in his silence. And I heard how deep the anguish and pride ran in my mother's Anzac Day eyes.

But now the Strait's peaceful sleepiness was a generation thick, the adrenaline of its troops on Australia's front-line long subdued. Instead I found relaxed dinners by kerosene lamp on beached prawners, walks up gentle hillsides with verdant gardens, and feasts of turtle, taro and tropical fruits spread out by generous villagers. Houses with cold showers were fringed with white gravel paths, and gardens sprouted hibiscus and bougainvil-lea. Pretty churches and porches of cottages were adorned with bright plastic flowers and coconut palms grew from shiny white sand. It seemed that pieces of Melanesia had simply floated into place at the top of Australia, where the mudflats of the northern islands became the coast of Papua New Guinea at low tide. A few generations before, these islander migrants had paddled their outrigger canoes from the north and the east to set up camp in the little visited paradise of the Strait.

Borroloola is a long way to the south-west of the Torres Strait, although decades after his removal John would discover that his family ties stretched into Queensland. His grandfather was born in Normanton. He never had a drink in his life, but they called him Publican Charlie. I grew up, like most Australians, knowing my place in generations of family. John had just his name. He says he was lucky to keep his father's name, John Moriarty.

It was his father's father's name too, and *his* father's before that. John always felt having his own name was something strong that he could hold on to. He felt sorry for other children whose white fathers had disowned them, and were given the surname of the place they were taken from—like Millie Glenn, from Glen Helen, whose father was a white station owner called Raggett, and Wally McArthur from McArthur River, the son of Langdon, the Borroloola policeman. People were called mocking inventions of names too, like Splinter Woody, Nosepeg John Carter who had a ceremony hole through his nose and the real name of Junkata, Twenty-Seven Johnny who had a lot of dogs, Billy Coolibah named after a gum tree, and Mussolini, the Yanyuwa's ceremonial boss.

John was glad for his name, but he would have also liked his own birthday. He was given 1 April, April Fool's Day. Many of the children taken away were given 1 April or 1 August, the birthday of horses. Kathleen told me John was born in the cold time. A letter from an administrator years later said it was 10 July. I've told John he should change the date to July. But he says who is to know if that is the truth either. And that it is too late now. The first of April is the birthday he has always had. He says he keeps it, too, as a reminder of what was done.

2

Belonging

narnu-yuwa
I belong to a place in the minds of my ancestors.

*My life fulfils the imagination of the generations who
came before me, and whose spirit I carry forward.
They prepared a special place for me, through
their hope, dreams and love.*

Day 2, Saturday 27 May 2006

*i*t is eleven o'clock by the time we drive in from the mine to Borroloola. We find Annie and Thelma at the fuel pump at the edge of town. Ready, anxious to go. We drive together to where more than twenty women are sitting with bags and mattresses on a cement verandah. They are all John's relations. Greetings begin again, and their hugs are warm and welcoming. I realise with relief I am not an intruder. I am a daughter-in-law, expected on the journey. Three other vehicles are loading up. We will drive in convoy. It is midday before everything is tied down on top of the cars, and we farewell John and Tim. I can tell John is happy I am doing this. Happy I am accepted. He feels deeply about it. My skin doesn't feel white here, and the women's doesn't seem black.

We stop at the store on the way out, buy more torches, load up with water and juices. A fifty-dollar note is all the town's cultural fund has distributed to each of the travelling women for the week. It's all gone by the end of the road out—given from the car windows to kids ambling along to the Borroloola Show. 'Can't go there with nothing in their pockets!'

We head out along the Carpentaria Highway. I have three passengers—Annie, Thelma and Dinah Norman Marrngawi. No personal names now—just kin names. It's the Law. A name may belong to someone who died. Can't use it. 'You call me Yuwani, and her too,' Annie says, nodding towards Dinah. 'Mother-in-law.' She moves on to Thelma—'You call her Baba—sister. She is Nangala. Same skin as you. She's your sister.'

31

Yuwani Annie starts to sing softly as we leave the town behind. The songs are in language. Baba Thelma and Yuwani Dinah join in. Gentle clapping of the beat. There is great contentment to be heading bush. Earlier this generation, the exodus from the summer camp would have been on foot, weeks of walking together stretching ahead. Catching small game, gathering seeds and berries in the cool of morning. Resting in the shade through the afternoon until the sting of the day's heat softened in the dusk, and the cooking fires burned down. Stories and songs providing a backdrop to the convivial preparation of food. Knowledge and nourishment being passed down with surety to every new generation, as clans crossed the land to sacred corroboree grounds. Now culture moves on wheels, and ceremony time is merely a pause in town life's sedentary routine.

We drive five hours, with a couple of fuel stops. One at Heartbreak—a crossroads stop an hour from Borroloola—the other at Hi-Way Inn, Daly Waters, at the junction of the Carpentaria and Stuart highways, north of Tennant Creek and Alice Springs. They are the same stops we made for years on the five-day drive from Adelaide, and on more recent fly-drive trips via Darwin. The convoy leaders are setting a cracking pace considering the state of the road. The sealed part of the road is narrow—just one car-width. The edge is loose red gravel. Even so, it is better to pull off the road to let semitrailers and cars with caravans pass. Safer to give them a wide berth than risk their tyres throwing up a stone to shatter the windscreen. Stock graze unfenced, and as twilight comes kangaroos may leap in front of the vehicle without warning. Eagles with enormous wingspans are already picking at recent road kill.

We drive into the western sky. The setting sun casts a golden glow of reflection on the top of the tree canopy that flanks the road. Trunks glow red. The sky turns powder pink above a layer of spongy blue on the horizon, deepening as the light fades. We are quiet in the car as the calmness of night drifts in.

We cross the Stuart Highway, and turn onto a dirt road in the dark. I have no idea how far it is to our destination, or even precisely where it is from here. Or where we'll be sleeping tonight. I am more than happy to leave the planning to others. I am open to whatever the week will bring. At the moment, I am a driver, a daughter-in-law and sister. It is an invigorating change from my life in the city, planning every quick-paced move of my job and the household.

The unsealed road is deeply corrugated. The car shudders violently, and neither slowing down nor speeding up seems to make it more comfortable. Two more vehicles have joined the convoy—meeting of the tribes has begun. We pull up in a line behind each other on the road verge. We wait an hour, maybe more, for another vehicle to catch up, then we make camp for the night at a railway siding. A clearing of stony red dirt by a train crossing on the main north–south line from Darwin to Adelaide. Tarps are pulled off the tops of vehicles, and swags and mattresses are thrown down in family and clan groups so we can go to bed. Everyone's too tired for dinner. There will be food for breakfast.

The vehicles are parked in a semicircle to flank the campground for thirty-five women and two small girls. The black sky is crystal clear overhead. No city lights here to dilute the darkness. I settle down into my swag, pulling the edge of my sleeping bag up under my chin. I throw the insect netting over my head to enclose my pillow. It is entirely pleasurable, a familiar feeling from the countless nights on the roadside, in dry creek beds and in the scrub, where John has taken us before.

The women chat and sing a little as they curl up on mattresses and swags around the fires. It is quiet here without the fights and noise of the town camps. Peaceful. 'No humbug here,' Annie tells me. It's like the exciting start of family treks out bush when they were just girls, and days of being together stretched out ahead. When the seasons and nature's cycles guided them to new hunting grounds, to birthing camps, or to life-affirming ceremonies. As they settle down to sleep, the dancing days ahead are the threads of anticipation that tie these sisters and nieces, mothers and grandmothers, aunties and mothers-in-law so strongly together.

Above us, the Milky Way is a slash of sheer silver gossamer, studded with diamonds. The stars of other constellations are in sharp focus, stretching far out into the heavens. Two trains blaze past in the night, sirens and headlights blaring as the signal bells ring on the road next to us. They pierce the total silence and wake some of the campers. There is quiet talking, singing. The pitch-dark explodes again a little later to the headlights of a semitrailer roaring past on the track, its load shaking with the corrugations. Then perfect quiet settles until dawn.

IN 1980 JOHN MOVED to Melbourne to head up Aboriginal Affairs in Victoria and Tasmania. The rush of falling in love had deepened for us both, but the inevitable crossroads of forever sometimes hung weightily overhead. I went to Europe for the northern winter with my flatmate Susan who, like me, was just a couple of years out of university.

I pondered the future in stony olive groves on Crete, in fire-warmed cafes in the Swiss Alps, by the mist-soaked canals of Venice. Donkeys laden with buckets of oranges trudged the Greek hillsides Susan and I climbed. The families who owned them served us olives and wine at plastic-covered tables. We stayed in whitewashed houses that basked under cerulean skies atop jutting cliffs. Below, boats nuzzled at wooden jetties on the sun-blue Mediterranean. Village fishermen threw silvery fish from their nets to the shore, and tiny eateries up the hill cooked them for us on fiery grills. Tomatoes and feta were full and sharp, and the honey of wild bees drizzled in sticky pools around tangy yoghurt. The sweet tastes of Crete seemed all the sweeter for the pared-down life around us.

ABBA and Queen pulsated in dimly lit bars in snowy alpine towns. Fernando's drums resonated with the whip of the sub-zero wind outdoors, and the thick, smoky heat inside. We slept in an Austrian attic under starched white quilts stuffed with softest duck down. We slept, too, on our bags in second-class carriages on chilly Italian trains, and rode the swell of the Adriatic in the stuffy bowels of the ferry from Brindisi to Piraeus. Old cobbled paths in watery back lanes of Venice led us to cathedrals on grand piazzas, and to red-orange sunsets that lit waterways where vessels had once plied the Orient. That winter was another world, in another dimension, and I could see Europe's history and spirit of place sat as a confident halo around its physical presence. I felt my own country was missing that connection entirely. Perched self-consciously on a foreign landscape, we were deaf to the beat of its ancient roots.

John also travelled to Europe that winter, although I didn't know he was there. He knew that Susan and I had vaguely planned to go to Amsterdam at the end of our trip, and he tried to get a message to me to meet him there. Our paths didn't cross, and John went on to Ireland in search of his father's family. It would be some time before I heard the dreamlike tale of his Irish homecoming.

When I came back to Australia in early 1981, I moved with the department to Sydney. I was sent for a while to Griffith, in country New South Wales. I lived in a hotel room in the main street, and walked the few hundred metres to the office each day. Field work in nearby rural towns and missions took me to places where Aboriginal people were trying to make sense of lives increasingly dependent on handouts. The cash tap that was gushing forth demanded little in return. As it always does, 'sit down money' killed self-respect and resolve. It was a case of all money, and little care.

A crisis was looming, all over Australia; a dilemma for everyone. For do-gooders who meant well but wore their hearts on their sleeves. For Aboriginal people like John who wanted to give people the tools to work for their living, the discipline to account for themselves, and the respect to continue their culture. For governments who had no workable plan, and no idea where to find one. The policies of free money would come back to haunt Aboriginal people over the next two decades, as they copped the blame for the irresponsibility that permissiveness inevitably breeds. And they'd be blamed, too, for the poverty that followed the inability of mainstream society to engage them.

People were hopelessly caught in the havoc two hundred years of white settlement had wrought. Pushed off their lands, dumped into missions and reserves, or left to the destitution of city ghettos, they had become the marginalised fringe. A sore on the fair complexion of Australia's international face. Aboriginal communities were drowning in a pitiful destruction that rendered children unable to read or write and saw families ripped apart by violence and abuse. Communities descended into squalor. Decency and respect flowed down the drain with last night's beer.

The self-management mantra continued to drone, but the statistics across health, education, employment, imprisonment and mortality were heartbreakingly cruel in their disparity with affluent, first-world Australia. The nobility of the fashionable notion—restore power to the people—could not excuse the desperation playing out on the ground. Those in the bush suffered the most and said the least. Their city brothers and sisters beat loudly on a drum of understandable if ineffectual frustration. People lived their difficult lives as best they could. They were stretched this way and that, like tired elastic, as the policies that governed them came in and went out on the whim of the latest political trend.

The six-hour road between Griffith and Melbourne was well travelled by John going north, and me going south, that year. We camped up on the Murray River with Yorta Yorta family, fishing for cod from the riverbank. The souvlaki was good at long noisy tables where we all gathered at Jimmy the Greek in Carlton. We danced at balls in the country, where giggling debutantes with shining dark eyes and lacy white dresses swelled the chests of their proud mothers and fathers.

By mid-year, we decided I'd move south to Melbourne permanently, and we borrowed some furniture and rented a small grey-walled flat in suburban Glen Iris. It felt like a test. Criticism still circulated among many of John's friends and professional peers.

Although some would apologise in years to come, their judgement was often hard to swallow. That John had separated from an Aboriginal woman, and that I'd rushed into a marriage with a fellow student and quickly divorced, added fuel to the fire. Too young and naïve, the impulsive mistake Alastair and I had made inflicted a sharp but relatively short burst of pain and regret on both of us and our families. For John, there was a lot of guilt that his marriage to Reta, an Indigenous woman from South Australia and herself a senior public servant, had ended just a few years after it began. To outsiders, theirs was a black marriage made in political heaven, and John's sense of having failed in the eyes of Aboriginal people and their supporters stirred a deep anguish in him. He was passionately committed to improving the lot of Aboriginal people, and he felt his differences with Reta were exacerbated by the deprivations and prejudices they had both known. When the marriage collapsed, John felt he'd sold out on a very personal level. There was a well of hurt and grief that ran more deeply than I could touch. I was too young and too close to know how to help. It would at times be a rocky pathway ahead.

Who knows whether the illegality of John's white father cohabiting with his black mother had forced them apart soon after John's birth, or whether his father had simply left one place for another. Regardless, the pressure we were facing forty years later, in a supposedly enlightened age, was heavily ironic. It was not the first time the race card had been played by John's peers and mentors. He'd been engaged to blonde Diana in the sixties. He broke it off when his mates warned him against cross-cultural marriage. The same men invariably went on to marry white girls. Their hypocrisy reflected their struggle to take hold of a future in Australian society, while not letting go of the Aboriginal identity deep within them. The odds were against them. Many, like John, would carry the scars of that battle throughout their lives, as would their families and loved ones taking the journey with them.

When we moved in together my career in Aboriginal Affairs ground to a halt, and I found a job for half my departmental pay with Australian Volunteers Abroad. We placed Australians with a conscience and a desire to help in developing countries. The issues seemed the same. Third-world communities who needed the key to a future more than the cash to squander it. Yet the Western world all over seemed more intent on scattering crumbs from their table rather than the knowledge to make bread.

The Melbourne Cup in November of 1980 started out as a rough day. As we opened our picnic trackside, the smell of the chicken and the fumes of the champagne left me woozy with nausea. I ate dry biscuits and drank lemonade for a week until we realised it was morning sickness, and in June 1981 our baby son John Timothy, called Tim, was born. I was twenty-four, and the depth of the emotion of his birth startled me. It was not just the euphoria of the event, which was to be expected, but the torrent of hoping and dreaming for this tiny person's life ahead that must rage without warning through every new parent's veins. A desire that made me ache inside with its intensity, to protect him and open the way with everything I had, to help him find his destiny. It was as if the writing began on my own life slate all over again, forever intertwined with his.

John's wonder ran just as deep, and in the moment of Tim's birth John told me he had the briefest glimpse of a very, very old face. He couldn't tell if it was where Tim had been, or where he was going.

We bought a cottage in Northcote, a suburb close to the city, and chiselled and scraped our way inch by painstaking inch through its dank wallpaper and tacky lino. The 1944 newspapers we unearthed under floors told us to eat lamb so the troops could eat beef. Melbourne was bitterly cold in June, and John, Tim and I crowded together in the one small room with a heater. John loved to lie with Tim all wrapped up on his chest. To curl him up in the crook of his side. He could protect him there. I loved to smell his bath-fresh skin, watch his gaze flick over colours in the room, and see him drift gently into placid sleep. We screenprinted long-neck turtles onto Tim's bedcover and curtains to celebrate his birth—a Yanyuwa child belonging to black and white worlds. We wanted him to feel the security John had in both cultures—not fall between them into the quicksand of confused identity. The turtles reminded him, as he grew, of the privilege of his Aboriginal birthright.

John and I married at St Faith's Anglican Church in Burwood, Melbourne, in August 1982. Tim cooed 'da, da, da' from the arms of my father in the front pew. We cried a lot at the altar. The sun shone down on us and our perfect day. We cooked barramundi in a steaming pit in our garden. We'd finished making the desserts with a kitchen full of friends and family at three o'clock that morning. The barramundi had been flown down by relations in Darwin, shiny-skinned and beautiful, on ice in some battered eskies. I've since realised these containers ply the airways back and forth between the bush and the city, their flimsy styrofoam basins groaning under the weight of parcels that keep people connected—fish, turtle, dugong and bush turkey, that come laden with longing to be together again. They arrived at our wedding with fresh fish and the gift of belonging.

We drove back up to the Gulf for our honeymoon. It took five days from Melbourne, in a yellow duco, black-roofed Ford Falcon with vinyl seats and no air-conditioning. Tim sweltered patiently in the back seat. We stopped every now and then to replace the wet face washer on his head. The windscreen was shattered by a stone from a semitrailer near Mount Isa, and after that the air came straight in through the front like the blast of a furnace.

When we turned onto the Barkly Tablelands, perhaps it was homing signals that sparked John's stories as we drove the last couple of hundred kilometres into Borroloola. His tales spilled over each other in a mixture of memories and anticipation. He talked about the beauty of the McArthur River and its creeks and billabongs; about how he had walked silently through its shallows with his uncles when he found his family again, and how we would fish from its banks with his aunties. He told me stories about all the people I would meet, about how I would love them and how they would love me. He said I was family now, and that meant I would belong just as surely as if I'd been born of the same blood. As the wife of a Yanyuwa man, and mother of a Yanyuwa baby, this was my place now, too. He joked he'd raided a Tasmanian tribe to take me as his wife. That we were 'straight' for each other in the old tribal way, because he'd gone a 'proper long way' to find me.

The sun was just setting as we drove along the dusty track into the Borroloola township with our baby. People walking along the roadside turned to see John through the open car window, and yelled to others nearby, 'John Mooriuddy. Eh, Mooriuddy!' We stopped every few metres. Men and women alike leaned into the car, pressing John's face to their faces, holding his head against their chests, crying to see him again; arms stretched through the back window to Tim's baby seat to touch him gently on his arm, his leg; hands extended to shake mine, in welcome.

We drove to the Yanyuwa town camp, and lifted Tim out of the car. Aunties and grandmothers wrapped soft ebony arms around our tiny boy of pale southern skin and creamy hair. They pressed my cheek to theirs: 'hello, my daughter', 'hello, my sister', 'hello, my granddaughter', 'hello, my daughter-in-law'. The men shook my hand warmly, averting their eyes as protocol demanded. I felt teary and grateful—for the generous welcome from my new family and, even more, for the very deep happiness John felt in bringing his baby boy home.

We pitched our tent next to Kathleen and Willie's trailer at Ryans Bend, about an hour's drive from town. Willie's dog Jack would bark longingly at bush tucker hanging out to dry in the trees. One morning he was halfway up a trunk, jaws about to close on a blood-streaked dugong tail, when Willie spotted him and bellowed at him to get down. The shouting startled him, and Jack lost momentum. Just at the moment of triumph he began an embarrassed backwards slide, claws finding little to grip on to halt his ignominious, accelerating descent.

Jack was a fine goanna hunter, and had the skin of a rhinoceros, wrinkled in the creases, his fur long gone from ticks and hard living. Sometimes when Willie could get to a phone, John would call from down south. He'd often ask after Jack.

'Your brother's okay, my son,' Willie would say.

Another time he would say, 'He's proper good that Jack, he attacked a snake and saved your mother.'

And most surprisingly of all, one time Willie would announce, 'He's proper good now, that brother of yours. Really good. He's got his fur back.' The hair restorer that Willie had washed him in was an inventive mix of kerosene and the laundry detergent Rinso.

Many a time brave Jack saved blind Kathleen's life from bush perils, losing his own eventually in one too many tussles with a poisonous king brown snake. Willie rang with the news. 'Your brother is gone, my son.'

That first trip back with Tim, the sparse savannah canopy gave only sporadic shade, and by September the sweaty build-up to the Wet had begun. The tent was thick with heat soon after sunrise, and tiny flies attacked the watery corners of our eyes as soon as we emerged to climb down to the creek to fill the billy.

Mosquitoes droned around exposed skin, and Tim's chubby body was soon red and mottled with bites and the heat. His bath was a big plastic bowl, where he sat splashing happily in the shade of the tent wall, the ubiquitous cool face washer soothing his little head. One of his eyes was infected shut from fly bite, and it hurt him when we bathed its swollen, crusty rim open in the mornings with warm water from the fire. Our first-aid kit was stuffed with the antibiotic cream he needed, and with tablets and syrups to treat the diarrhoea and vomiting we knew he wouldn't escape; these chronic childhood illnesses are rampant in Aboriginal communities all over Australia.

I was ill too, a deep rattling chest infection with a roaring fever and splitting headaches. Dugong fat made me vomit violently, and tiny specks of black sand flies, *kirdil*, caused welts that within hours turned to infected yellowy blisters which itched and burned for days. I learned which part of the dugong to eat, and made John promise that he would never again take me to the estuary at dawn or dusk when the *kirdil* excreted their stinging mucus.

We washed in the creek, keeping an eye out for snakes by the banks. We kept fresh food from town on ice until it melted. Then we soaked dried beans and stewed them in a pot on the fire with vegetables like onions and pumpkin that could sit around for a few days in those temperatures. Les James was growing tomatoes and watermelons on dusty ground nearby. He was a white man who'd lived on a borrowed landholding for longer than most people could remember, and his fresh juicy produce was sought after along that road. Kathleen and Willie shared turtle and dugong with us, and catfish was a favourite grilled treat.

In the cool relief of evening, we sat around the fire. Flames licking shiny light that would catch your glance and gently prolong it in a quiet space where time slowed down. We listened to Kathleen's stories of the night sky. Sightless by day, at night she could see pinpricks of light from the starry galaxies of her ceremony stories. She lulled Timmy to sleep with soft songs of her Dreamings from those stars.

That first visit for baby Tim was his naming time. We knew his skin was Balarinji, son of Bulanyi, John and Nangalama—my given skin. 'Skin' is a system of classifying people. Eight skin groups for men, and eight for women, stretch across the centre and the north of the Australian continent, linking people to land and ceremony. It embeds them in the comfort of family relationships of obligation and privilege: giving and receiving. Skin determines who can marry each other, a pragmatic necessity in earlier times when purity of bloodlines ensured healthy births among nomads who lived on the edge of survival. Sociological mapping of skin in tribal times was a complex web, a sophisticated and highly successful way to bind families and people together. It was an unforgiving system too. Wrong-way marriages were punishable by death, and deformed babies resulting from bad blood unions were often put to death. The survival of the tribe demanded it.

This visit, it was Tim's bush name we were waiting for. The name that would tell of his totem, his place in the geography of the Gulf. John's name is Jumbana. His totems are kangaroo and Rainbow Serpent. His land runs from Centre Island across to the east of the McArthur River, almost to Managoora, through to Balbirini south-west of Borroloola, and to Hodgson Downs in the north-west. Mine is Wanujubi, linked to the deep-sea groper. John's tribal brother Samuel jokes that I was given it because I have 'big mouth, talk too much', but really my links are to Groper Dreaming on South West Island. I belong to a story that begins

44

in Queensland when the Groper decided to travel west, and at Nyamarranguru on South West Island her head and fat became a Dreaming. If the custodians of the Groper ceremony go there and strike the rock that is her head, groper in the surrounding sea will be plentiful.

Old Tim Rakuwurlma, whom we named Tim after, would decide our baby's bush name. Our wriggly, active toddler sat on old Tim's crippled knee for three days, hardly moving. On the fourth day, he was declared Baniyan, cheeky (or poisonous) brown snake. As the grandson of the omnipotent Rainbow Snake spirit ancestor, Baniyan embodies a powerful intersection of Yanyuwa ceremony lines. Tim's belonging to land stretches from Centre and Vanderlin Islands to the Limmen Bight in the west.

I could see a well of knowing in Tim Rakuwurlma. He was over ninety when he named our Tim. He would sit on the ground at his camp, shifting slightly now and then to change the weight on his withered limbs, or pour tea from the billy smoking away on the fire. He found enough satisfaction in family around him, the spirit of a life well lived in the Law, and some food and shelter. His memory was a chronicle of the twentieth century in the Gulf. He remembered the visits by the Macassans to his family's islands when he was a small boy at the turn of the century. Long before the British colonised Australia, these adventurous, swarthy fishermen began sailing the short distance between their home port of Macassar in the Celebes (now called Ujung Pandung in Sulawesi, Indonesia) and northern Australia.

The Macassans came to trade, bringing technologies like the dugout canoe and metal nails for hunting dugong. Supplying rice, tobacco and the alcoholic drink arrack. They set up cooking camps along the coast and on the islands to process the trepang— marine cucumbers—they harvested from coastal mudflats and deeper waters. They returned home in prahus laden with pearl shell, turtle shell, horns from buffalo, dried shark fins, pearls, sandalwood, and the metals tin and manganese. Sometimes they took Aboriginal men with them on their voyages. They had plied those waterways as recently as old Tim's boyhood, and their camps are still marked today by the towering red-wooded tamarind trees they planted, and the stone piles where they hung their trepang boiling pots.

For the Yanyuwa, connecting with the Macassans changed their horizons. It began to challenge the way things had been, when clans had moved from place to place—a few months at one camp, a few weeks at another, returning to the old camp the following year, when the seasons had replenished the place and it was fresh with life once again. Now the stone-lined wells the Macassans dug at their cooking stations provided permanent drinking water and the enticement of a more settled life. Availability of water often dictated the time to move camp. Now the Yanyuwa were able to stay longer in their seasonal places, even into the late Dry, when natural waterholes had dried up and the Macassans had sailed home.

The new, stronger dugout canoe of the Macassans was safer than local bark canoes, could travel further along the rivers or out to sea to hunt dugong and turtle, and had more room to transport bird eggs and chicks, fish and shellfish. Aboriginal people were hired by the Macassans to work as labourers, they learned new skills and added to their knowledge of technologies for their island and coastal lifestyle. Temporary camps became semi-permanent, and while European settlement of southern Australia was more cataclysmic in its demolition of traditional life, in the remote north the Yanyuwa were just as surely seeing the beginning of the end of tens of thousands of years as nomadic wanderers.

When I think back to those three days when I watched Tim Rakuwurlma with our baby on his lap, I feel in awe of the generations of spiritual life on the Australian continent he embodied. As well, I feel deeply sad and frustrated to have witnessed the wafer of time that separated the rich and bountiful bush living he had been born to, and the impoverished town existence of his life's twilight. In the blink of this old man's lifetime, the secret sacred world of his generation, and all the generations before him, was flickering passively, silently, towards its ending. Late twentieth-century Australia would mark the point of no return. The riches of mind, body and spirit that Aboriginal people had painstakingly nurtured and passed down for thousands of years would fade from memory and practice for ever. The spectre of this passing brought for me confronting questions and an unease about the folly of denial among those of us who embrace an Australia that only began when the British arrived. The feeling of not knowing what is lost until it is gone.

It was an understanding that I would come to later. I would be lying if I said that travelling in the Gulf on that first visit was a Utopian revelation. Often the scorching, uncomfortable days with a baby stretched into nights of exhaustion where I'd climb into bed in the tent to scratch the bites on my grimy body, and fall coughing and feverish into a fitful sleep. I would wake in the early hours, worrying to the point of teary panic about whether Tim's vomiting and diarrhoea were more sinister than our presumptions about how to treat him from our medicine kit.

The steady calm and patience of John's mother and Willie left me wondering. They had no vehicle in which to drive to town for food and, in any case, the scant money of their pension every second Thursday wouldn't go far at the ludicrously overpriced community store. Profiteers had a licence to write money off the backs of Aboriginal people in communities throughout Australia, often taking possession of each month's social benefit to pay the arrears. The new fortnight's supplies would be entered in the sales book, and the cycle of debt and extortionate buying would continue.

Kathleen and Willie depended on younger people and families living at their outstation or nearby to share their bush tucker when they could get some—fish, dugong, turtle. Or beef when stray bullocks were killed. When there was food to eat, they ate. When there was none, they drank water and tea and waited. The waiting had its base in traditional life, when elders were respected and cared for, their wisdom and knowledge recognised and valued. But by the early eighties in Borroloola, the system was beginning to disintegrate, drinking was accelerating, and old people often went hungry and cold.

As a young wife and mother, the world of my new family was beyond my comprehension. I had seen disadvantage in my research days with the department. Borroloola, though, was a different sort of deprivation. It ran deeper and wider and seemed forgotten behind the desolation of those endless roads in and out of the Gulf. It was as if different rules applied because there were no windows in. Authorities in town seemed unmoved by the endemic sickness and poverty. By the hunger. People's passive acceptance of it all made it sadder. It was humbling to see the communion and joy of family in the face of it.

John's blending back into the Yanyuwa was seamless. He loved to sit cross-legged by the campfire, shifting the billy on a glowing log, stoking the coals to throw the fish on. He was in tune with the subtle shifts in the bush around us. The way things smelled, the sounds at dawn and dusk—insects with wings that rubbed softly together, birds that squawked the daylight in, the splash of a particular river fish. The soft-edged tracks of a croc on the sandy bottom in shallow estuary waters. John's uncles Mussolini (Musso) Harvey Bangkarrinu and Leo Finlay Wurrawurra were there that trip. They were the ones who'd taken John back into ceremony when he'd returned to the Gulf almost thirty years after he was taken away. Musso was a crocodile man—*mardumbarra*—and the soul of the Gulf of Carpentaria ran through his veins. The heartbeat of his land brushed against me when I sat near him, heard his voice in language, and watched his big strong hands fix an outboard, cast a net or throw a spear. He was all bodily strength and deep spirit. Musso and Leo were big Law men, John said. While it is not for women to know, I could imagine the leaders they were at sacred corroborees on moonlit ceremony nights.

The heat was wrapping around us like a swampy blanket by the time we headed south. The thought of cooler weather was overwhelming. I found it hard to think of anything else. The goodbyes, though, when we left Borroloola with baby Tim that first visit took even longer than the hellos. John said his aunty had told him off when he'd left once before without seeing everyone to say goodbye. Tears flowed from family, not so much for themselves and the separation, but for the sadness they felt for us and our imminent lack of connection. To family, to land, and to the all-pervading Law that sets the order of life.

The yellow Ford let us down on the journey home. One hundred kilometres out of Borroloola the car overheated, and we spluttered into Heartbreak. We poured more water and the white of an egg into the radiator, hoping to glue up the leak that had sprung up somewhere in the engine. By the time we reached Mallapunya, not too far down the track, we realised that sixty kilometres per hour was the speed when the leak would blow. So we crawled to the railhead at Alice Springs to board the train.

We drove almost thirty-six hours without a break day and night. I tried to give John a rest on the first evening, but it was not even an hour before my eyes began to droop and it was too dangerous to continue. We slept an hour or so on the roadside, then John got behind the wheel again and we limped south. Tim sat patiently in his baby seat. He had taken his first steps at Borroloola, and wouldn't take any more until we had settled into a new life in Adelaide.

3

Giving

ngulhu
Generosity and understanding my
obligation are the same.

Generosity is a given: it is not a special thing,
it is only what is expected of me.

Day 3, Sunday 28 May 2006

*W*ay before dawn, Yuwani Annie rises next to me on her mattress, and wraps a blanket over her head to keep the cold air out. A hacking cough won't let her sleep. She is recovering from flu and chews Log Cabin tobacco which makes it worse, but it is a small vice in a life as hard as hers. She starts singing songs in language. They are ancient ceremony songs. Others join in. They call to each other in loud voices, willing the camp awake. Gradually piccaninny daylight comes—the time just before dawn when the sky begins to lighten ahead of sunrise. The evening star is the last diamond left hanging. It becomes the morning star, shining still, as daylight comes.

It is chilly. We collect firewood, dragging logs along the rail siding. Their dragging gouges streaky lines in the sandy ground. Fires are relit and flames are soon spiralling skywards. When the fires have burned down we cook sausages, chops and steaks in shifts on a smoke-blackened grill plate. They are shared along with bread and sauce, boxes of oranges and apples, and billy tea. This is unusual abundance for breakfast. A piece of cold meat from the night before, or more likely nothing at all, is the norm back at the town camp. I have found out that the Central Land Council will look after logistics for the week, including the food. It is so good to see these ageing women eating enough. Their pension cheques at home are just as likely as not to end up providing grog money for others in the family. I can see they appreciate the unaccustomed sensation of full stomachs, and there is plenty of cooked meat left over for the next few hours of travel.

I ask Yuwani Annie if I can take photos of the lines of swags and chatting women.

'No,' she tells me. 'No photos. You'll just have to write it all down. But you can't write down the ceremony business. You will see full ceremony. You can't tell anyone else. Just keep it for yourself.' Then she changes her mind. 'It's all right. You can take photos here at the camp. But not at the ceremony ground.' I move around the Yanyuwa camp, taking photos of the senior Law women as Yuwani Annie directs me. My generally reliable camera jams repeatedly, and I change the settings. I hope it is working. There is a vivid, honest beauty in the women's faces in my lens. Their skin drinks in the early morning light.

We begin to pack up the night's camp. One of the Borroloola women is dancing up near the road for a laugh when a car rumbles past. Hysterics from the group when she is sighted. She plays to the audience and dances up towards the railway track. The crossing bells suddenly start to clang, a train whistle sounds, and the group descends again into raucous laughter. Singing in language breaks out. Anticipation is high for the days of ceremony ahead.

There is little English being spoken. 'I have to teach you Yanyuwa,' Annie says.

'John is my true son, my daughter-in-law,' she keeps telling me. 'When his mother pass away, she tell me to look after that boy.'

'Then look after me,' John joked with her yesterday.

We drive an hour to Top Springs fuel stop. I use the public phone to tell Security at the mine where we are, and that we are setting out on the track south-west to Kalkaringi. I can't tell them the exact destination—I don't know. Half an hour out of Top Springs, the convoy pulls up. A tyre blow-out on the car with the trailer. Women pile out to sit in the shade under a tree on the roadside. There is no shortage of expertise with the jack, and the wheel is changed in minutes.

Along the highway, monsters of eagles and crows are feeding on kangaroo carcasses. They are bold. They retreat just a little, heads cocked, waiting for the car to pass. Vegetation is sparser, although still green as we head towards desert country. A lot of rain came way down south this Wet.

Songs continue in language in the back seat. In unison, then in harmony. The modulations, if not the language, are becoming familiar, although the corrugations of the badly chopped up road make it hard to hear.

We arrive at the turn-off. A makeshift sign reads: WOMEN'S LAW MEETING. A few kilometres down the sandy track, and more than twenty-four hours since we left Borroloola, we arrive at the ceremony ground. A huge circle has been cleared in the scrub—a field of rich red sand. Already the desert women are dancing. There are camps dotted around the perimeter. Later I do a rough count of more than two hundred women scattered within their groups. Tribal, clan and family camps with a few drivers or workers. A massive truck with a freezer trailer has carted in food for the week. A generator drones by its side. More than twenty four-wheel drives are parked near the camps.

We follow our convoy in, and pull up on the edge of the circle behind the others. As I get out of the car, there is sustained hissing from my front and back tyres on the right-hand side. Both are deflating, pierced by a stick in the scrub we've just driven through, on the side of the ceremony ground. The stick is still protruding from the back tyre. Fortunately,

I meet Francene, a powerhouse of a young woman from the Tennant Creek group. She works for the land council, and is here for ceremony too. She tells me her father died when she was twelve, and she is one of four sisters. Clearly she can do anything. She gives me a lesson in changing big, heavy-duty tyres. I am covered in red dust and pouring sweat by the time we get them changed. Francene is patient, helpful and no doubt amused by my incompetence. As the logistics chief for the week, she must have plenty of other things to do.

Our camp is being set up in a treed clearing just off the ceremony ground. Yuwani Annie chooses a place in the inner circle to put down the tarp that she and I will sleep on, and sends my niece Kathakatha to unroll my swag. I tell her it's no problem, I can set it up. 'No, Narna (Aunty),' she says. 'Kukurdi (grandmother) told me to do it.' Family hierarchy matters here.

Fires are set and lit between the sleeping groups of three or four women. Food bags arrive with meat, powdered milk, carton milk, Weet-Bix, porridge, tomato sauce, tea and coffee. Dinner and breakfast. Meat is quickly cooked and eaten on a slice of bread, tea is brewed, and the camp settles down as the light begins to fade. Women call from one side of the camp to the other. Logs are thrown on the fires to keep them burning. Our fire is not far from the side of my swag, and it is uncomfortably hot. I will ask Annie if we can move our tarp further from the fire tomorrow night.

I have prepared myself for the night. I put a bottle of water, my sweater and a torch in the side of my swag between the canvas and the netting. I tuck my glasses in the side of my pillowcase, and slide my shoes under the front tip of the swag. Crawling insects or reptiles are less likely to find them there and surprise me in the morning. I wriggle out of my outer clothes before I sleep. I have used the water in the back of the car to splash my face and clean my teeth. The mint tastes luxurious.

It is the same black star-filled sky tonight, although the breeze is not as cool. There is a lot of talking around the camp. I roll eventually into a shallow sleep, feeling a long way away, missing John and the children. That two of the children are adults and one almost makes no difference to the hollow feeling in my stomach. The penetrating quiet of the bush makes me feel sharply alone.

WHEN WE CAME BACK from our first trip to the Gulf with baby Tim, Adelaide was the place we put down roots. John had a job in the Department of Aboriginal Affairs there, and I was in a career drift. I'd written and recorded segments for Radio Australia—on women's affairs, the Franklin River conservation debate, Aboriginal issues—after Tim was born. But most of the time I spent caring for our baby. We moved in with Billie and Bruce Holland while we looked for a house. The Hollands were a big-hearted white family who'd taken John in when he was kicked out of the boys' home at sixteen, even though they'd had barely enough room for their own kids, and certainly no cash to spare. Now they welcomed John back, with Tim and me to boot.

Billie Holland is a woman with a beautiful spirit, in her eighties now, who loves John as fiercely as if he were her own. Always did, John says. Her husband Bruce was a 'knockabout bloke' according to John. Was at the pub most nights until closing, but never said a word against John in all the years the Hollands put a roof over his head and a meal on the table. Their daughter Wendy is as blonde as John is dark, and as close to him as any sister could be.

I was surprised that elsewhere in Adelaide, the ugly face of racism occasionally reared its head. A real-estate agent showed us a quiet flat in leafy Leabrook, which we agreed was fine. The rent was no problem on John's senior public servant's wage. On returning to the office to sign the lease, the agent's superior took one look at John and said the flat was gone. I wanted to take him on, but John said it was always easier just to let it go.

I noticed on trips out of town John would always get me to go in alone to ask for an on-site van or a motel room. I complained that I was tired too, and how about he go in sometimes. He said if he did, they would be full.

Sometimes it was very close to home. When we bought a house in fashionable St Peters, our elderly neighbour Gladys knocked on the front door. She was probably in her late seventies.

'Roslynne,' she said, 'what nationality is John?'

'Australian, Glad,' I told her.

'No, I mean, where is he from?'

'Australia,' I repeated.

I could see her wringing her hands a bit, skirting around the question she wanted to ask. Trying to place John's features and skin.

'Actually, he's Aboriginal,' I volunteered.

'Oh,' she said slowly. 'I thought he might be Indian.' Pause. 'Or a Pacific Islander.' Or anything else, seemed to be the inference.

'No, Glad. He's Aboriginal. And the baby is too.'

She didn't say any more.

We went away for Christmas just as the beautiful wisteria vine at the side of our garden was spilling a torrent of purple blossoms along our verandah roof. We came back to find Glad had come into our garden and cut it off at its root. Glad hadn't liked an offshoot wending its unruly way into her lemon tree. A stony silence from over the fence suggested she hadn't liked us wending our way into her suburb either.

Then she had a motive for a change of heart. She knocked on the front door.

'Roslynne,' she started. 'You know how you said John was Aboriginal, well, does he do any of those *really* Aboriginal things, like throw the boomerang or play the didgeridoo?'

'Yes, Glad, he does both,' I told her.

'Oh, that's good,' she said. 'Because my relatives are coming from Germany, and I'd like to do a little show.'

I closed the door, sat on the hall floor, and laughed in disbelief. It was even funnier when John said he'd do it. As it turned out, the relatives, Hans and Karin Appel and their son and daughter, were nothing at all like Glad. John did the didgeridoo and boomerang show, and we took them throwing spears in the park for good measure. They welcomed us the following year to their apartment in Stuttgart, but in the fourteen years we lived in St Peters, we failed to strike up a friendship with Glad. She did, though, continue to provide comic relief on occasions. When Tim took up drums, his practice was punctuated with eighty-something Glad pelting our garage roof with rocks.

A few months after we settled into our house, John's mum and Willie came down from Borroloola for a holiday. It was hellishly hot, in that searing Adelaide way. An inferno of northerly winds off the desert brought a February of raging bushfires across South Australia and Victoria. The house was old and the air inside was stifling. We sat often on the cement of the front verandah in the evenings, Kathleen and Willie cross-legged on the ground, Tim curled up on a knee. I was pleased our expanding black family was in full view of Glad's windows. During that visit, some Borroloola women came to Adelaide for a dance festival, and they arrived one afternoon, pouring from the door of a minibus. Glad's fingers must have ached from holding open the crack in the venetian blinds of her sitting-room window.

It was strange for John's mum and Willie at our place. Nowhere outside to light a fire and throw on some fish. Sleeping in a stuffy, closed-up house, with locks on all the doors and windows. Few familiar birdcalls in the morning, or rustlings of nocturnal animals to give sequence to the passing of time and light. They were quietly gracious, patient. Appreciative of the smallest thing. Kathleen gradually learned to feel her way from the front bedroom down the hall and around to the bathroom and kitchen at the back of the house.

John took them into the city, helping his mother to visualise new things she could sense but couldn't see. He took them to the boys' home in Semaphore where he'd grown up, and introduced them to his brother-friends who'd grown up there too. They came with us to the port, where the salty air smelled familiar like the Gulf. We took photos of Tim in their arms and of us all together. The pictures began to bridge the years of empty album pages. John had put together more and more of the pieces of the Borroloola side of his life since beginning his journeys back to the family. Those few weeks in Adelaide filled in some more. I felt so sad for them all. For the gaping silence of the time taken from them. John was insistent in his questions, yearning to know more about the life he'd been forced to leave behind.

Kathleen told John her mother was Elsie, a Yanyuwa-Marra woman, who belonged to land stretching from the Sir Edward Pellew Group of islands in the Gulf to Roper River, west of

Borroloola. In the early part of Elsie's life, she'd never seen a white person. She'd lived a fully bush life with her family on their traditional lands. Clans of about twenty-five people used to camp together as extended families on lands of male lineage. The men hunted big game like kangaroo and dugong, the women caught turtle and goanna, and gathered bush seeds and berries. The catch would be prepared and cooked in the cool of evening at places with sweet (fresh) water. It was around these cooking fires that children learned bush stories, ones to make them laugh and ones to make them scared, teaching them how to live safe and happy lives. The old people passed down the *kujika*, the songlines of the Dreaming, so the land would be cared for, the seasons would be in balance, and country would be nurtured for every new generation to come. Once a year, the whole tribe—around three hundred people at the time of European contact—would come together for ceremonies that bound them all in the sacred Law.

During the latter part of Elsie's childhood in the late nineteenth century, Europeans arrived in the Gulf. They were mostly deviant characters, criminals running from the law. Borroloola people still talk about the time when Europeans first came. They call it 'the wild times' before people 'quietened down'. Their families described events of appalling violence. Their dispassionate way of relating the atrocities doesn't mask a sickening reality. People tell in graphic detail about relatives shot for sport like wild animals, about children being killed like dogs, pummelled to death with sticks like the ones used for hunting goanna. They remember babies being beaten to death and set alight with kerosene.

The Yanyuwa are surprisingly forgiving about the time when European and Aboriginal people didn't understand each other, 'couldn't talk in each other's language'. They admit that some spearings were because countrymen thought the white-skinned

Europeans were evil spirits. Spears were no match for gun-powder, however, and it is hard to know how widespread the genocide was. Whites didn't include blacks in the populations they counted, and rarely recorded the scalps the hunting parties took.

And the Europeans wrote a different history. This was the time when explorers, pioneers and cattlemen 'opened up' the wild, inhospitable frontiers of Australia's vast outback. Killings of natives were referred to as 'dispersals', punishment for the innate savagery they said inspired attacks against settlers. In fact it was loss of land and resources that sparked the conflict, but to ignore that was convenient for colonial expansion—indeed, necessary for it. A divine right to civilise the 'uncivilised' excused the sins the God-fearing newcomers committed against their 'heathen' brethren. Those falling under the guns were seen as miserable specimens of the stone age, remnants of a bizarre and worthless culture, when in reality they were the custodians of the longest continuing human tradition in the history of the planet. And someone's beloved mother, sister, father or child. Their blood, and the barbaric circumstances of the shedding of it, will forever stain the pages of Australia's colonial history.

Police had been stationed in Borroloola since the 1880s, although their arrival had had little to do with Aboriginal families like Elsie's, who were mostly still living out bush. They were sent to control the whites: horse and cattle thieves, murderers and violent drunks who were evading jail in Queensland and other parts of the Northern Territory. Even though the shootings declined, Borroloola's lawless reputation deservedly remained. In scenes more reminiscent of the American wild west than British Australia, there was plenty of hard drinking, shooting practice in the streets and stores being held up. The story goes that one drunk European killed himself by galloping a stolen horse around town before being thrown against a tree. When the jail opened in 1886, all nine prisoners were European. By the early 1890s a handful of Aboriginal people were incarcerated, mostly for the traditional practice of lighting fires or payback killings.

After the turn of the century, cattle theft and drunkenness were the reasons for most arrests. The Aboriginal prison population swelled. Kept naked except for a belt and tassel, they were herded into work gangs, chained at the neck with padlocks and at the ankles by rings. People insisted they were only killing cattle that roamed on their traditional lands, that they were hungry, and were simply living off the resources of the bush, like they always had. The settlers had no patience for this argument, and demanded swift retribution for hunting their herds. Many simply took the law and a rifle into their own hands.

Yanyuwa families like Elsie's were better protected from early European contact than other tribes in the region. In the early 1900s, they were still paddling their dugout canoes between camping places on their islands and the coast, some eighty kilometers from the township of Borroloola. By 1900, the violence of the wild times was over as the European population had dwindled to nearly nothing. In 1901, whites numbered just six. Pastoralists replaced the itinerants, and the physical isolation of Yanyuwa lands made them less attractive for these cattlemen expanding their empires. Sometimes Yanyuwa chose to trade, like they had with the Macassans, bartering fish and dugong for tobacco. Generally they kept a low profile. They could disappear at will in landscapes they knew intimately.

Kathleen said her father, Publican Charlie, married into the Gulf tribes. He was a tall, strong Kalkadoon man from Normanton in Queensland, initiated into the Arukun group on Cape York, with Garrawa links to the Rainbow Snake Dreaming of the Gulf. He worked on vessels that plied the coasts of Queensland and the Territory, and he probably met Elsie after he sailed up the McArthur River to Borroloola on a voyage to bring supplies to the growing number of Europeans travelling the overland stock route from Queensland to the Northern Territory and Western Australia.

Kathleen was raised in bush camps by Elsie and Charlie, learning all the languages of this crossroads country of many tribes. She became fluent in Yanyuwa, Marra, Gudanji, Binbingka, Alawa, Waanyi, Garrawa and Jingili. She learned all the songs and ceremonies that her mother and aunties passed down. They taught her by the campfire, and on arduous treks across country— the same journeys the spirit ancestors made in the Dreaming, the creation time. She whispered and smiled with John on that visit to Adelaide, cried too, gesturing with her expressive hands, telling her boy about his grandfather and grandmother in the old traditional times.

Later in the year Kathleen and Willie visited, the Australian Wool Corporation launched our family design business. Our idea was to build on the long-neck turtles we'd screenprinted onto Tim's baby bed linen, and create a line of Aboriginal-designed textiles for fashion and furnishings. We called it Jumbana, one of John's bush names. Later the brand would become Balarinji, our sons' skin name. We began with a sketchy dream to share the beauty of Aboriginal imagery and culture with other Australians. And it was a defiant statement to an Australia that had tried to destroy John's links to his culture. We set out on a journey of the heart.

On our honeymoon trip to the Gulf, we'd collected bits of the landscape from riverbeds and gullys. Sticks, charcoal, river pebbles, chunks of sticky clay and flaky ochre. The colours sang in harmony in our hands. Nature blended rich and subtle, light and dark, cold and warm in an effortless, spontaneous mix. Grasses on the roadside resonated in a breezy, shimmering blur as the car sped past brown-tinged sienna stalks, feathery tops the colour of straw, and stony-lime tufts of wispy desert ground cover. Blue-purple mountain ranges stretched across red-sand horizons that began in mornings of lightness, and ended in the rosy weight of settling dusk.

We squeezed gouache colours from heat-soft tubes, mixing the runny, colour-laden pigment to match what we saw around us. Brushstrokes of small colour slabs in books of white parchment would become the palette to take us through the next twenty-five years of creating a new visual language of Australia. The culture songs of Borroloola and pounding feet of Yanyuwa dancers on ochre sand sat at one with these hues and tones of the land mother of the Dreaming. The culture, the colour and the voice of the country were loud inspiration to fire our dawning creative ambitions.

We ploughed our total savings of $12,000 into starting the business. It had seemed a massive amount of money at the time, but it was all gone in five minutes. We had no business expertise at all, and we'd decided we didn't want government money with its ties of dependency. We had no formal design training either. Just a vision we couldn't keep a lid on. We raced blithely forward. Pregnant again by now, I walked up and down Melbourne's Flinders Lane to buy rolls of superfine wools, silks and cottons. I scoured phone directories to hire printers who would translate our sketches to fabric. I took a flight or overnight train from Adelaide to Melbourne every few weeks with toddler Tim, wheeling him in and out of warehouses and print shops, the pregnancy ticking away as the months went by.

John plugged away at his day job in government service, more and more disenchanted by the stagnation of weary, ineffective policies. Somehow we met the September 1983 launch date for our textiles, and we were tenuously on our way. Dotted patterns of tiny *nynka* bird tracks, cave-etched silhouettes of *ancestor* spirits and stamped circles of sweet-water camp were the earliest patterns to give visibility to the beginning of our ideas.

The day after the launch our second son James was born, three weeks premature. We'd barely made the hour's flight back from Melbourne in time for the dash to the hospital. This perfect little brown-skinned baby brought a fresh rush of love to the family. I was a mother again, and it was an emotional time of gratitude for this healthy new baby. Maybe it is the natural high of child-birth that sends mothers' brains somewhere in the immediate aftermath. I floated in a hazy space, watching wind in the leaves and clouds in the sky. My fudgy mind wandered in protesting counterpoint to the strain of our rocky developing business.

Before James was a week old, I was poring over files and accounts. We had two small boys now, and our lack of capital for the business began to bite. John held down his government job, and we worked together in the evenings and into the night once the children were in bed. John would draw, and I would colour the images. We diverted much of John's wage to the snow-balling business. It was gathering pace, but not commercial success, and it would be eight years before we could take a cent of salary from its meagre coffers.

Susan and Doug Pike and their two young sons lived a few doors down in St Peters. Sue worked at the children's hospital, and I met her when two-year-old Tim fell and hit his head. We discovered we were neighbours, and a child's outpatient check was the start of a lifelong friendship. We devoured nectarines, peaches, spinach and sweetcorn from the Pikes' garden. Money was so tight in the business that I often joked with Sue she saved us from scurvy. Like me, Sue was juggling a job and a young family. We laughed till we cried when she discovered cobwebs in and out of Doug's socks and underwear she'd left on the line for a few weeks; we laughed some more when John called Doug to see my latest baking disaster—'You've got to see this, mate'—hurling my poorly risen chocolate cake like a frisbee to Doug at the front door. When Tim sliced his toe on a broken bath tile one afternoon, John and Doug took him off to the clinic. The doctor explained he would sew it up just like Mummy sewed on Daddy's shirt buttons. Tim looked mystified, and John and Doug had enough to dine out on for years to come.

Sometimes we could see the lighter side, but near insanity prevailed as we mortgaged the house to the hilt to secure the borrowings the company needed to keep trading. There were many Mondays when we wondered if we would still have a roof over our heads by Friday, let alone if we could feed ourselves and our children. It wasn't for lack of interest in our work. We were featuring in magazines, television programs and newspapers. What started out as our quest to celebrate the blended heritage of our children had struck a chord in the national conscious-ness. Adelaide fashion designer George Gross bought our silks and wools, Budget Rent-a-Car commissioned uniform fabrics, bedding superbrand Sheridan created an outback collection with our graphics, and tourists began to buy our scarves and textiles that exploded with the landscape colours of our travels out bush. We were simply suffering the fate of many new small businesses. We had no idea how to price our services or products, we'd never heard of profit margins, and the demands and excite-ment of designing left little time for the accounts.

A long-suffering man who would become our accountant, mentor and friend, Richard Wishart, stepped in to save us from ourselves and from our bankers. He was not quite in time, though, to prevent a manic decision we made the December after we launched, when James was just three months old, to accept an invitation to exhibit our work in The Hague, Netherlands. An indescribably generous travel agent in Adelaide advanced us the fares and we set off, battling both the logistics of travelling with babies in the freezing cold European winter and my postnatal exhaustion with its rollercoaster emotions.

In June the following year, we took our textile collection to Tokyo to launch with the International Wool Secretariat. It was a short trip and my parents came from Tasmania to look after three-year-old Tim and nine-month-old James. It was too soon, and I felt physically ill to be away from them. I burst into embarrassed tears in a quiet, formal Tokyo restaurant because I missed them so desperately. The stress was building.

John's senior job with the government had its own pressures, and it was normal for him to bring home for lunch or dinner twenty or so people from out of town. Finding the money to pay for it was one thing. Trying to stay sane with the children and the business and cooking for crowds was another. One weekend there were twelve for lunch on the Sunday, and twenty-two for dinner on Monday night. The boys were still tiny. On the Tuesday, having organised child care, I flew to Melbourne to talk to department-store buyers. I raced from a day of meetings to a pasta restaurant in Carlton to meet friends. A few minutes after I eased into a chair blackness closed in, and I woke several minutes later on the floor. I had apparently been fitting.

My friends helped me back to the hotel and called a doctor in. There was nothing to find. I was very scared. I flew home, had some tests, and took stock of the pattern of things. I hadn't stopped, really, since giving birth to James more than a year before. Whenever I'd felt at exhaustion point, I'd kept going on ever-stronger black coffee and chocolate, sleeping just a few hours either side of midnight. I'd been breastfeeding James during the 1983 America's Cup yachting campaign—the one Alan Bond and John Bertrand won for Australia. James would stir for a feed just as the live coverage from America came on air. I am sure there are a few other nursing mothers around Australia, with children in their mid-twenties, who associate that patriotic win with breast milk. After his feed, I'd pop James back down at 3 am, and keep working until Tim woke around six. At the end of a day with two babies John would come home, we'd eat, read Tim a story, settle James, and start on the drawing, painting and paperwork all over again. Perhaps if it had been only a business, and not a dream, I could have taken a different view of the destructive pace at which we were travelling. But something beyond our power was sweeping us along.

I didn't collapse again, but for months on end I would wake around one in the morning, feeling anxious, crying, gasping for breath, my heart thumping and racing. I had premonitions of disaster, convinced I would die before morning and leave our children without a mother. Afraid to go to sleep, things were spiralling downwards. I panicked in crowded public places, and avoided friends. I was only twenty-eight. I was too embarrassed to admit to a breakdown, but as James neared his third birthday John took leave, we battened down the hatches around the business for a few weeks, scraped together the money to hire a campervan, and drove north into the healing balm of the red desert on our way back to Borroloola.

4

Meaning

ngalki
My inner spirit is my substance in the world.

*My inner spirit holds the unique beauty and meaning of
my being. It is the essence of who I am in the world.*

Day 4, Monday 29 May 2006

*i*t feels like 4 am when we stir at the desert camp. It is dark, and cold. Annie sits up on her mattress next to me, and calls across the camp in language. Everyone starts to stir. It's actually after six. The sky is the clear, translucent indigo of pre-dawn. It gradually turns to the familiar night-and-morning sponge cake of palest pink and powder blue layers, until the sun rises to bleach the colour and the morning star away. We get up and stoke the fire. The billy is filled with water and put on the coals to boil. We fossick around for Weet-Bix, powdered milk.

Before we can eat, we are called to the ceremony ground for the first of the rituals. Before coming here, Annie told me just once, but with authority, that I am not permitted to write about any content of the ceremonies or the sacred objects. No detail. I can only say that Annie takes me with her in the line, and tells me: 'This will make you strong'. It is solemn, simple, deep. I can feel it. I have sensed moments of similar spiritual calm in foreign places, burning a single candle in a quiet moment in another country's cathedral. But this is just a big circle of red sand, inside a ring of desert grass and scattered, spindly trees. In my own country.

The dancing, the singing and the beat of clap sticks start soon after. The other mob first.

'We respect them,' Annie tells me. 'It's their country.'

They are the same sacred songs handed down for thousands of generations to those who have the authority to receive them. They have deep meaning. They encapsulate the

73

Law. The rules of the culture to keep everything right. Season follows season with abundance. The species procreate, and people are in balance with the earth, the sea and the universe. There is renewal for the human spirit. We are quiet. Respectful. Looking from a way away.

The wind is whipping the sand around the dancers. It is *a-Mardu*—the south cold-weather wind, Yuwani Annie tells me. I like its lemony sharpness on my face. It counters the intensity of the sun that I know will rise by midday. It is early winter in the desert, but the days are still hot. Annie tells me it is good for me to come to these ceremonies. Really strong. All women. Really good.

Annie and the others tell me who everyone is. 'Your mum, *kujaka*; your sister, *baba*; your aunty, *narna*; your mother's brother's daughter, *kathakatha*; your father's brother's daughter, *kulhakulha*; your mother-in-law, *yuwani*.' I start to remember the words more often. 'You call her Kujaka, she's straight sister for your mother.' Only family here. No dislocation or ambiguity. Clear and straight. No exclusion. The Law has joined these women of many bloodlines. There is no fear to include, to embrace with unconditional permanency.

I feel a tranquillity, a strength, from the non-negotiable rules of connection around me. Inclusion is a powerful thing. I am a sister, aunty, niece, daughter-in-law. I wait, and Yuwani Annie tells me what to do. Every step of the way. She looks after John for his mother, and that includes looking after me. I feel emotionally nurtured, supported. In Sydney, I look after my mother and I look after my children. Here, I have simply stopped in the middle: they all look after me. It is deeply calming.

I quietly ask Annie when we can talk about the book. Later, she tells me, when there's time.

I borrow the satellite phone in the freezer truck. I call the mine. There is no way I will get back for Friday's flight. Ceremonies won't finish until Friday, and there will be an overnight stop on the way. Probably back Saturday. No flight from McArthur to Darwin until Monday. I get a message to John to change my flight, to ring the office and cancel my Monday meetings in Sydney. I leave the satellite number for emergency calls. It lets me relax a little more. I'm a phone call away if my family suddenly needs me.

We are called to the ceremony ground. The women from Central Australia call the Borroloola women over. Protocols. We are seated on the ground on one side of the dance area. The ritual starts. It is feminine, sensual, lyrical. There is parody, symbolism, charade. Rhythm and form. Irony and humour. It is expressive, sophisticated. Pared down to a richly devised essence. 'Very important one,' Annie whispers. 'Strong Dreamin'.' It is a long time out there on the ceremony ground. Yet the minutes and hours merge, as if time is not passing at all.

It occurs to me that the invisibility of the occasion is remarkable. The modern sophisticated nation I live in has no idea that the singing of the continent it sits on continues in the heart of its landscapes. We newcomers have barely scratched the surface of the power of the land we occupy to inspire and nourish. To stir the senses and lift the heart. We see the stillness of dawn at the ocean, the cacophony of summer cicadas, the ripples of red dunes in the desert, and marvel at Australia's natural endowments. But we are far from being at one with it. We sip at its physicality, when we could gulp from the well of its spirit.

Back in our own area, the camp is collegiate. Women enjoying time when time stalls. I look at my watch, expecting it to be late afternoon. It's 2 pm. We sit, talk, laugh, sing. We sew strips of cotton for ceremonial headbands for tomorrow. The crisp-edged wind that was blowing across the ceremony ground this morning is blocked out of our camp by a pile of leafy windbreaks. It is still and hot. I move to the shade to sit with one group, then another. They all have stories to tell me. Guidance to give me. If I interrupt their contemplation, or ask brazen questions, they don't tell me so. They excuse my ignorance. They speak gently to me. Sharing food, laughs and truths about their world. They take me carefully with them on this journey of the heart and mind. I am profoundly moved. And grateful.

At dusk, it is not the swirling dust that is stinging my face now, but the smoke from the campfire. My eyes are raw and streaming. Yuwani Annie starts to sing. Someone taps a spoon against her enamel mug. Rhythm and song are never far from the surface, here at the ceremony ground. They are always ready. Yuwani Annie tells me the story of her song. It is the song of the dugong hunters in the islands, when the turtle goes up the shore to lay its eggs. It is the Green Turtle Dreaming place, and the ancestors always collected eggs from that country.

In this down time from the ceremony, a big gambling circle is playing cards for money in the torchlight. It is animated, noisy.

It is night-time. I miss my children again. The separation and isolation is more brittle when I lie down to sleep. Something has brought my emotions bubbling to the surface this week. Annie lies on her mattress under her blankets, and tells me about the Dreaming.

I think back to the old ways, she tells me. *Not much about the missionaries. But we're not so much different. A little bit the same. Aboriginal people were created too. People ask how come we black. Anyway, Adam and Eve were a little bit black.* She continues, *I read the Bible, and it's the same: traditional owners fighting for their land. There's a tribe in one land, another one fighting for another land.* She weaves the two histories seamlessly together. *Dreamin' make us. Ceremony too. God give the ceremony to people. Some part of Adam and Eve countrymen were black. We believe in our own way, the Dreamin'.*

She talks to me about childbirth. *The child spirit stays around in their clan country. The child spirit cries out to find its right mother and right father. The mother and father dream about the child spirit and it comes to the mother.*

About the spirit world. *A spirit is* ngawulu. *Like a shadow. A good shadow. Follows you. I stay in my place and a shadow comes through the door, and no-one's there, but I know the spirit is there to guide me. Invisible.*

And about the stars. *The Milky Way is Dreamin' for my mob. Grandfather, father and brother. My clan group has this Dreamin'. It's a sacred ceremony—men's business. We know it's theirs. We have strong story too for* warrawiji, *evening star, morning star.*

The Dreaming is an ever-present force in Annie's life, as it is for all the senior Law women at the camp. It pervades the everyday, the secret and the sacred. It is a concept outside European frames of thinking. It is the Law and it is the stories that were given to the ancestors in the creation time, and passed faithfully down from generation to generation ever since. The Dreaming is in everything, it is an essence, it is in animals, plants, birds, fish, people and the elements. It is in the songs and ceremonies, the names for all the land and the sea. When the spirit ancestors travelled the Australian landscape in the Dreaming, they made the songs, the maps for knowing country. They made the marks for body paint, so when people ochre up to dance they are respecting the Law that never changes, continuing the traditions that will keep everything right. People must protect country so that its Dreaming stays safe forever.

Annie and I have swapped sides tonight. Her mattress is now by the fire. She was cold last night. This is better for her. I feel more comfortable with a cool breeze drifting across my face.

There is no washing allowed here in the ceremony time. Just face and hands. I have cleansed and moisturised my face this evening. Glossed my dry, cracked lips. Three small girls around the camp wanted their lips glossed too. Maria, Natasha and Stephanie. They like being pretty. The same as little girls the world over. My hands are sandpaper. I have wads of red dirt under my nails despite gouging them out with a skinny stick.

Night fires are dotted in a semicircle out on the ceremony ground. It makes me think of Vikings.

STRESSES AND STRAINS BEGAN to fall away as we drove north from Adelaide in the winter of 1986. The open road is reached so quickly from this elegant city perched on the desert's edge. With each kilometre, the colours of the land swell and deepen from sandy to red, and the sky gets bigger and bluer. We sliced our favourite salami for lunch by the roadside, piling it between bread with chunks of sharp cheddar. The boys ran out some of the energy that had been brewing in the car. They were five and almost three. With a four- or five-day drive stretching ahead, family tempers would inevitably ebb and flow with the fatigue of distance.

The campervan we'd hired became our home for the weeks of travel, and it laboured under the weight of us. It groaned a little on the hills, and more than once its belly became lodged on sandy mounds in the middle of the road, its wheels spinning in the air. Some vigorous digging with a garden spade, and we'd be on our way again. The vehicle was of little use as the four-wheel drive it purported to be, but the pop-top was a novelty. Tim and James loved to lie up there in their bunks, watching the stars and the moon scatter light across the night sky. They listened sleepily to John's stories of the bush around them.

As we drove further into the heartland of the red centre, nights and mornings became crisper. In this land of searing winter daytime heat, the night temperature plummets, and we often woke to ice on the ground. We huddled over the campfire at breakfast, warming frosty hands around steaming mugs of billy tea and hot chocolate. The sunlight, weak at first, beat down more strongly by the time we took the first break of the day on the road, the warmth seeping into car-sore bones and muscles.

By the time we made the turn-off to Uluru, Ayers Rock, we'd been travelling for a few days. There are no showers where you camp off the road, but buckets are fine for a thorough scrub and rinse. A shampoo and blow-dry are of course out of reach, and mirrors are best left at home. In the shop at the turn-off I noticed Judy, a mum from Tim's class at school in Adelaide. I tapped her on the shoulder, said, 'Hi, we've met at our sons' school.' She looked at me for a moment and said,

'I don't think so,' and, taking her small boy's hand, walked away. I looked at John over my shoulder, with his three-day stubble and fraying shorts, and grubby-faced Tim and James swinging noisily around his legs. And saw my own dishevelled reflection in the glass of the drinks fridge doors. I guess I shouldn't have been surprised by Judy's response. We became cordial acquaintances in the years to come at school—neither of us ever mentioned that moment at the turn-off.

At Uluru, Tim and James scrambled a little way up the slope of the famous icon, perching under an overhang together. We mixed colours just below them: ochre reds, vermilion, scarlet, cadmium orange and magenta in a hot rock palette; stones and slates for spiky grasses and chalky charcoal; cerulean blue, cobalt, indigo and violet for the transition of sky; mauves and ultramarine bleached with white for the view to Kata Tjuta, the Olgas. Our brushstrokes reflected the brilliant desert light.

Leaving Uluru, the heat of afternoon had relaxed gently into dusk as we drove into Palm Valley near Hermannsburg, one hundred and forty kilometres west of Alice Springs. Gus Williams, a local Arrente man, came out there to camp with us. The peace of Palm Valley seems heightened by spectacular landforms and Red Cabbage palms that are hundreds of years old. More than three thousand of these palms remain as relics of prehistoric times when Central Australia was much wetter. Palm Valley is the only place in the world where they grow, and they form a lush oasis in this gorge. The valley carries a weighty solitude, perhaps soberly conscious of the aeons it has witnessed. Standing inside its rim, I was drawn down into its echoing amphitheatre, into the symmetry of its ridge-framed basin. Its crisp silence and pure desert air invigorate the spirit. I would be surprised if anyone who goes there is not touched on some level by the power of this land to stir the soul. It is Gus Williams's mother country, and he is at one with it. After we'd cooked on the fire and eaten by torchlight, Gus began calling dingoes from the escarpment. They howled back to him. The magical conversation between Gus and the distant dogs continued well into the night.

We kept driving north, camping well off the highway in dry, sandy creek beds. There have been violent murders and unsolved disappearances on desolate Territory roads over the years, and John always said he never feared the wildlife, only wild people. He liked us to be out of sight of the road. There was plenty of firewood, and a fridge in the van made it easier to stock up occasionally on fresh food to cook on the coals. Each day without walls faded our connection to city trappings, reduced things down to the essentials of food, rest and travel. Sleep became deeper; sight, sound and smell became keener. Thinking was clearer and I felt the pervasive healing that nature brings.

We called into the art community of Yuendumu, where painters were dotting acrylics on glorious canvases, impervious to camp dogs and the elements. The paintings from this region of the Western Desert, and further along the road in Papunya, are believed by many to mark the greatest abstract movement in Australian art, and were at the time beginning to grace the walls of fashionable galleries and collectors in America and Europe. The permanent manifestation of stories previously made in the sand for ceremonies and later erased, these rhythmic, meaning-laden works marked the start of a phenomenally successful international market in Aboriginal dot art.

At Yuendumu, I realised afresh that John knows just about everyone everywhere. If he doesn't know the individual, the quintessential questions of 'Who is your mother?' and 'What is your skin?' never fail to find the link. No strangers out here. Just countrymen. The net of skin and kin throws its mantle over family from one corner of the continent to the other.

The final camp before Borroloola was in the scrub near Tennant Creek. We cooked on a smoky eucalypt fire, and bedded down on our swags under an orb moon that floodlit the landscape in silver. In the dead of night, a feral cat darted through the camp in a furry, shimmering flash. In the early hours of the morning, I lay on my stomach watching the moonlit dew on spikes of desert grass, coated in the brilliant light. Those tranquil moments return often to my mind's eye.

We drove the seven hundred kilometres through to Borroloola the next day. It was James's first trip back to the family. Like Tim, he was going for his name, Jawarrawarral, dugong; for his belonging. John's mum was living in town this trip, so we headed straight in. John had shot a bush turkey on the outskirts for Kathleen to cook: her favourite bush tucker, along with left-handed wallaby, goanna, echidna and turtle. She took Tim in her arms, then James, meeting her new grandson for the first time. John described him to her: his big black eyes, golden brown skin, his sunshine grin. The boys' other grandmothers and aunties took them in their arms too, holding them tightly in their love. A lot of small kids were running around the camp. As with children everywhere, it didn't take long before our two were racing around noisily with them.

My mother and father, Nancy and Owen Langham, had decided to make their first trek from Tasmania to the Gulf with us that winter, and they met us in Borroloola. They'd driven up the east coast of New South Wales and Queensland, and into the Territory from Mount Isa. They loved John as a son, and wanted to meet his family. Mum had found her church group in Devonport was occasionally vocal on the plight of Aborigines, and not always well informed. She took the fight to them, and loved to quote her son-in-law. 'A gentle man' she called John, and vowed she would never stand by to hear a word said against him or his people. John used to chuckle that once or twice she told him, when he'd enquired how her day had been, she'd been 'working like a nigger'. It was the era when the second line of 'eeny, meeny, miney, moe' was changed to 'catch a *tigger* by the toe'. Mum was often deliciously and innocently politically incorrect, and John loved her for her lack of artifice.

We set up camp with the van at the Crossing—a narrowing of the McArthur River at the eastern side of the Borroloola township. My parents parked their own kombi van further along the bank, as under local custom John wasn't permitted to speak to his mother-in-law unless through an intermediary. It was a special time for all of us. Mum gravitated to the local church, and got to know a number of the Borroloola women, especially Bella Charlie Marrajabu, who was an active Christian. Dad wandered along the river, threw a line in, and spotlit crocodiles at night. They met Kathleen and Willie, and we all ate heartily together from the coals.

The Crossing, where we camped, is on the road to Queensland, three hundred kilometres along the track, and is passable to traffic only in the Dry. In the Wet, the small outrider communities of Garrawa families and clan groups who live across the river are isolated from town, as they have been since European settlement. Despite decades of patient asking, successive Darwin-centric administrations have left these people cut off from supplies and services for several months of the year. With bush tucker all but hunted out and no access across this major waterway, how on earth are these families meant to survive and function? The inaction within government towards this, and towards a myriad of other injustices that make daily life nearly impossible, is beyond belief.

Locals often fish from the low road-bridge at the Crossing, and drunks sunning themselves on the rocks are taken by crocs from time to time. On this visit, more than twenty years ago, the big salties—estuarine crocodiles—were not so often seen far upriver around people, and the boys played in and out of an old bathtub in the shallows to cool off, John keeping a watchful eye. At night, further downstream, it was a different matter, and our evening walks with a spotlight picked out wide-set pairs of red eyes lurking in the shallows. The river's banks were high enough to keep these majestic but ruthless predators from our camp.

We had some luck fishing that week, some large barramundi—the succulent dense-fleshed river fish that runs in fresh and brackish waters across northern Australia in the Wet. Catching some in the Dry was a treat. We packed up the catch, and drove a couple of hours to the Wearyan River for a weekend camp. We set up swags on the white sandy foreshore of a waterway that begins over a rocky outcrop as a cascade, then flows gently downriver towards the Gulf. Paperbarks, cycads and pandanus palms line banks where crocs lurk—twenty years ago they were freshies, the longer-snouted fish-eating cousins of the salties. A few years later bigger Wets would bring the salties further upstream, and it would become too dangerous to swim in the languid pools of the Wearyan.

Some of the men killed a bullock for fresh beef on the way in that night, and we threw both the fish and the meat on the coals as the sun was setting. It was extraordinary. It encapsulates in my mind all that is beautifully simple and full of heart about sharing a special meal with family. The delicious fire-seared fish and chargrilled meat fed the whole clan bedding down for the night on the banks of the Wearyan. The fishing, the travelling away from town, setting up the camp and the quiet chat around the aromatic cooking fire lulled us all into the settling dusk.

Later I realised why people love a chance to leave town and camp sixty kilometres upriver at the Wearyan. Besides its scenic beauty by flowing water, it has a special place in the hearts and minds of the Yanyuwa because it is a deeply significant cultural site, and their last major ceremony outside Borroloola was held there. In 1950, hundreds of Aboriginal people travelled for Law business from distant Queensland to the east, and Roper River to the north-west, to assemble in the bush with the Yanyuwa for the last time. The memories must be bittersweet for people at the Wearyan, as the cessation of ceremonies out bush marked a devastating change for the Yanyuwa that would see the steady, irreversible disintegration of their spiritual life on the land. Ironically, the lush and prolific Wearyan played a major part in the circumstances that led to a breakdown of culture that was not apparent until there was no return.

For centuries, Manangoora, on the Wearyan, was a favourite seasonal camping place for the Yanyuwa. The river provided a reliable freshwater source, and it was only fifteen kilometres from the sea. This meant there was an abundant diet of mainland as well as saltwater foods. Yams, wallabies, goanna, sugarbag, cycad palm nuts, unlimited quantities of fish. Managoora's position on the river gave people great mobility too—they could paddle up and downstream to hunt turtle and dugong, collect bush food, trade goods and meet for ceremony. Camping by its shores, I could see John as a baby with his mother in this beautiful place. Perhaps curled up in a basket she'd woven, sleeping in a shady cranny, close by her side. I could imagine the cooking fires of times gone by, gentle smoke wafting through the foliage as the day's catch was thrown on the coals. As the season began to change, an eye would have been kept out for the storm clouds marking the build-up to the Wet, signalling the time to retreat from the floods of incoming king tides.

It is a place that is rich in archaeological remains. Stone artifacts indicate the place was used well before the Macassans introduced steel and glass. There are extensive middens of shellfish being eroded from the riverbanks, attesting to the antiquity of the deposits and the long history of people making camp there. Older Borroloola people remember Manangoora as 'one of the big places' where people camped, moving on to other places they had responsibility for at other times of the year. Younger people remember being there most of the time, and this is the central theme about the point of no going back for the Yanyuwa, and all that it came to mean for cultural loss, dispossession and future chronic disadvantage. The relative immunity of the Yanyuwa to Europeans of the wild times, even to the early pastoralists, through their geographical good fortune came to an end at Manangoora. It was here, on their own land, that the bounty of their special place appealed too strongly to Europeans, and the enticements of a white lifestyle sowed the seeds among the Yanyuwa of an irresistible and irreparable demise.

Horace Foster was a European—some say a Fleet Street journalist—who found his way to the Wearyan in the 1920s. He set up an enterprise working the saltpan that flooded with seawater each Wet season. He chose it because of the ready-made workforce of Aboriginal people camping at Manangoora. They raked the salt into heaps, and bagged it ready for river boats to come and take it away. It suited both Horace and the Yanyuwa perfectly. The salt was ready to be collected by July in the Dry, when the saltpan had dried out from the flooding of the Wet. By October it was too hot to continue, and the tide would come back in to flood the area again. By that time, the Yanyuwa were in any case ready to move to a drier summer camp.

As time went by, people gradually began to spend longer at Manangoora and less time at other locations. At Horace's homestead, they learned new skills in cooking, gardening, making things from horsehair, how to speak English. Tobacco, sugar and tea were in plentiful supply, and processed flour offered a far less labour-intensive alternative to the traditional practice of soaking and grinding cycad nuts for making bread. There was a level of interdependence developing between the station on one side of the river, and the Yanyuwa camp on the other. But the relationship was still part of its era, and Kathleen told John his aunty was buried alive at Manangoora for being unable to carry one more bag of salt. Women have bad memories too of the sexual demands put on them by the boss and other European men who stayed with him.

Horace Foster accidentally shot himself and died in March 1941. There are a number of versions of this story. A favourite says his shotgun jammed, he grabbed it by the barrel and whacked it against a tree, and it went off. The bullet lodged in his groin. Yanyuwa men set out by canoe, paddling downriver to the sea, along the coast and into the McArthur River, all the way to Borroloola. They found Sister Ruth Heathcock, an Aboriginal woman from Point McLeay in South Australia, who was the nurse there and married to the policeman. They paddled her all the way back to Horace. Sister Ruth always maintained she saw guiding spirits in front of them, leading the boat. But three days had passed, and it was too late. Horace had lockjaw—tetanus—and gangrene had set in. Sister Ruth knocked out two of his teeth to feed him, but to no avail, and they buried him near the homestead. Two of Horace's children with an Aboriginal woman, Jim and Rose, were taken away like John. Rose went back to Borroloola once or twice. Jim lives in Adelaide and hasn't ever returned.

The salt works survived the passing of Horace Foster, and by the late 1940s a patrol officer reported 'approximately sixty natives' were living on the opposite side of the river to the station, by then home to Andy Anderson, a European who lived with a series of Aboriginal women and 'half-caste' children. Manangoora had become the first semi-permanent Yanyuwa settlement, and marked the beginning of the Yanyuwa 'coming in' from the bush for good. At the time ceremonial life continued, a discreet distance away from the European homestead. Bush tucker was still eagerly sought after too, and when European supplies ran low the cycad nut equivalent of flour was relied on.

Borroloola women have strong memories of the time when people started 'settling down'. Manjikarra Jemima says life was good during her childhood at Manangoora.

When I been small I used to stay at Manangoora with my mum and my uncle. I been grow up in Manangoora. We used to go out hunting, used to collect bush tucker. Like that munya. Like a passionfruit, but different. Cycad. We been living on that bush tucker all the time. We never used to have sore, or sickness, because we been living on bush tucker all the time. Eat all them wild cucumber, bush tucker, grow riverside. All that we used to eat. And sugarbag, dugong, kangaroo or fish.

All the old people used to get ration, little bit tucker, like sugar, milk, porridge and flour. We used to run out of food. We used to eat bush tucker all the time.

My uncle and my aunty, they used to work for salt, for Andy Anderson. They used to collect that salt.

But Manangoora was not sustainable as a semi-permanent settlement. In 1948 a cyclone stirred up a tidal wave that destroyed its gardens, and made the previously productive soil too saline for growing vegetables. By now, there was no going back. Bush tucker could no longer feed the large number of people who were living at the Wearyan for longer periods than a nomadic camp could support. Other camps had long since been abandoned, and a reliance on European food and other commodities since the turn of the century had taken its toll on the ability of Yanyuwa to continue to live off the land.

The Wearyan remained a ceremony place, though, even after the last major Law business out bush finished. Into the 1960s, people continued to visit the place because of the spiritual significance of the cycad palms, associated with the Tiger Shark Dreaming. The ancient story is that the Tiger Shark cared for cycad nuts and palms to the east. He had a fight with fish who were making fun of him, the trevally, the large eagle ray, the hammerhead shark and the black-tipped shark. So the Tiger Shark ripped the cycads from the ground, and quietly travelled west, in the depths of the sea, with a bundle of dried nuts on his head. He placed a small parcel to the north at a reef he named Wurlma (Vanderlin Rocks), and tried to place more at a nearby island he named Nungkkariwurra, but a rock wallaby refused him angrily and told him to go south to the mainland. Tired from carrying the bundle of cycads, the Tiger Shark travelled up the Wearyan River just as far as Manangoora, and threw the cycad nuts, the sacred food, everywhere there, calling out the names for the country and for the cycad palms he was erecting. He took his eye and placed it to the south, and created a well he called Dungkurramaji, which is still its name today. The Tiger Shark then met a Spirit Man at Kalalakinda to the south, and gave him the power songs for the poison the cycad nut contains. So that place at Manangoora became Ma-wirla, meaning a place where there is plentiful food able to feed many people who come together there.

Ceremony was critical to keeping stories like the Tiger Shark alive, so the Wearyan would continue to be spiritually strong. A momentous blow to culture hit in 1979, when some of the key cycad palms were cut down by pastoralists for cattle yards. The Yanyuwa were sad and angry. Not just for the sacred trees, but because the whole area has such binding spiritual and emotional ties for them. This act of irreversible vandalism is a callous reminder that not even thirty years ago these Europeans in the Gulf were unconcerned with the Yanyuwa way of seeing their homelands. With a few exceptions, that continues to be the case.

When we travelled out to the Wearyan during that trip in 1986, the wounds from the severed trees were still raw. People nevertheless would always seize the opportunity to go there. With the paraphernalia we carried around, it struck me how simply people were able to travel. Just a rolled-up mattress and a couple of blankets. A billy for the fire. We seemed to be encumbered by city comforts that faded into obsolescence out there. The lights and gas stove and folding chairs were left in the van. The fire and a blackened pan were all that we needed. And a fishing line at the ready.

Tim and James loved the sandy foreshore at the Wearyan. We floated upstream a little way on air beds, paddling with our arms and legs. Looking back, I often think it was foolhardy. That the enormous crocs we saw on future visits to the Wearyan could have been lurking below. Sometimes a big Wet brings them up, perhaps an old one is displaced by younger, more aggressive males. The old wounded one is as desperate and dangerous as a croco-dile can be. But this visit we were oblivious to the possibility, and the tepid water on our sun-drenched skin was a balmy change from the southern winter we'd left behind. The boys loved to roll and wrestle in the sand by the water, and I was brushing James's skin off one morning when we noticed red lumps on his body. It wasn't a rash from the sand, but impetigo—school sores. He was covered in angry, weeping blisters that itched and burned until he sobbed from the pain. A highly contagious bacterial condition, it was typical of the debilitating ailments our healthy children would inevitably catch on our years of visits to the Gulf. I was always frightened for them, and sorry that so many local kids suffered such chronic, preventable illnesses.

Even more worrying that trip, and an aftermath of the impetigo, was a lump the size of an egg that came up in James's neck a few days later when we were halfway across the ten-hour overland route to Darwin via the Limmen River. He was not even three, and I was sick with thoughts about what this grossly swollen lump might be. He was feverish and quiet. We kept dosing him with paracetamol, and wiping him down with damp cloths. We pressed on to Darwin Hospital and waited anxiously in emergency, to find it was an infected lymph gland. It was not as bad as we'd feared, but was serious enough. They wanted to admit him to put him on an antibiotic drip, but we'd heard horror stories of Aboriginal children from Borroloola dying of unknown causes in Darwin Hospital, and we insisted they give him an injection and let us get on the road. James lay on the floor of the van under the flow of the air-conditioner, and his temperature gradually fell and stabilised. We stopped at Tennant Creek on the way south for another shot, and once again in Alice Springs before we loaded the van on the train for the trip home to Adelaide.

5

Love

kina palirra
Thank you, you are there.

I love you as you are. You are there. It is enough.

i t was a colder night last night. My hips ache from the hours spent sitting on the ground. Shifting from awkward crossed legs to one leg stretched out, to both legs stretched and arms locked behind on the ground. Effortless for the others. They have patient stillness, waiting to be called. Protocols.

Yuwani Annie's voice rings out in song this morning in the pre-dawn stillness. It is still dark. Her contralto tones are stronger every day. I begin to recognise the melodies. Today she calls out a message across the camp.

'This big land, Australia. It's big enough for *ev*eryone.' She lingers on the '*ev*ery' in 'everyone', stressing the first syllable.

Annie as orator is not a random occurrence at the ceremony week. She is fulfilling the traditional role of a 'loudspeaker'. In Annie's younger life public speaking had a central role in bush life, when the announcer spread news across the camp and provided a platform for local politics. Loudspeakers would address clan groups settling down for the night, and again when they woke in the morning. Sometimes it was to suggest when to move on, where food would be and what ceremony would happen soon. Other times it was to publicly air a problem or a grievance, and find a solution. If conflict couldn't be resolved, a formal fight might be organised. One traditional fighting ground of the Yanyuwa later became a football pitch. Loudspeaking stopped when bush camps were replaced by houses, because voices were blocked out by their walls. Out here in the desert this week, Yuwani Annie is the embodiment of how close to the surface traditions still simmer—and a reminder of what an effective mechanism loudspeaking must have been for a wandering tribe whose survival depended on unambiguous communication. The public airing of dissent, consensus and intent provided a clear platform for collective decisions.

Billys are boiled and sweetened tea is quickly poured to warm everyone up. We sit close to the fire, piling on more logs to stoke the flames.

We are waiting for ceremony another day. Sunday, Monday, Tuesday—the Borroloola women still wait patiently. Dancing tomorrow, Wednesday.

'We respect them,' Annie tells me. 'It's the Law. We let them do their dancing first. This their country.'

By mid-morning we are sitting in the centre of the ceremony ground. Watching solemn, sacred dancing. Women's stories linked with men. The assurance of generation following generation resounds in the rhythms of their bodies and their voices. Relationships at the centre of the meanings. There is support, nurturing. Only the top layer is obvious to me, but Annie whispers an explanation. I can feel the power of sadness, release and regeneration. There is absolution in the stories. Forgiveness and release. 'Frees people up,' Annie tells me. The biblical links are unexpected. But there is nothing to suggest this is any missionary aftermath. It is the basic humanity of failing and forgiveness. That such emotions are displayed and resolved spreads its strength around those dancing and those seated on the desert sand.

I go out this afternoon with the camp support women to cut and carry wood. Enough for the thirty or so fires continuously burning for the two hundred women scattered around the ceremony ground in sleeping groups. Chainsawing, sledgehammering, cutting tree trunks with axes. Loading onto trailers and onto vehicle roofs to distribute around the ceremony ground perimeter. I am grateful for the exercise, the chance to stretch my limbs after the hours of quiet sitting. Rubbish bags need to be distributed, water containers refilled, and food bags delivered with chicken, onion, pumpkin, broccoli, rice, more Weet-Bix, tea and sugar.

It is red termite country where we go out to find wood. Towering ant hills like pillars. Scrubby trees are mid-green against the clearest cloudless sky, subtly paler at the horizon.

Today is hot. Francene, as adept with the sledgehammer as she is with car axles, asks me if I have any sunscreen on. My face is neon red. The more from lugging wood. Yes, I tell her. Thirty plus. This is harsh country. My eyes are now constantly watering and sore from dust, ash and smoke. But no flies, no ants. Unlike summer, when the desert swarms with them. Francene has good advice about the dust. Leave it on your face. It keeps the sun off. It mixes with my sunscreen. Back at the camp I sit on my swag and scribble in my diary. I drape a sweater across the back of my neck to keep the late afternoon sun off. The sun is stinging still at 5 pm. It's the time of day in the desert winter when the chill will spread in surprise in an hour or two with the falling dark.

In the evenings my heart aches for John. For his mother who lost him when he was just four years old. For the deep love these women have for him, that was denied to him when he was little more than a baby. For the pain he had, and the courage he found to be the person he is. The heart and positivity of his life. These women grieve for him still. They have cried for sixty years for one small boy of an

Aboriginal mother and an Irish father. Bulanyi. My husband, my children's father.

I ask Annie and Thelma separately if there is a good time soon to talk about the things for the book. Like love. Annie shakes her head. Difficult here. The Business to do here. Can only talk a little bit. Then she tells me something that blows me away.

'We don't say "I love you",' she tells me. 'We say *kina palirra*. It means "thank you, you are there".' Powerful. Unconditional. I love you as you are. You are there. It is enough.

I want to ask her about another big topic. Grief. But I don't need to ask. This evening, just after dark, Thelma whispers to me that a message has come through on the satellite phone for one of the families. Must be bad news, she says. Someone goes off to ring on the truck radio. They are driven back in the support team's Toyota, bringing news of the death of a close relative. Soft crying starts in the family groups settled for the evening. Restrained. Quiet. Their bodies shake with the sobbing. It subsides.

Annie, the loudspeaker, calls across the camp. 'We have sadness in our hearts. Yes. But we must give it up, give it up, give it up.'

A young woman has died in Darwin Hospital. She had a kidney transplant, but the family got her drinking again and she got sick. But they didn't know she was so sick. No-one told them she was so sick. A shock.

THE DICHOTOMY OF OUR lives continued back in Adelaide after that 1986 winter in Borroloola, separated only by geography from the source of the philosophy that was driving our design work. I felt sorry that most Australians could not experience what I'd discovered about our country. What lay beneath the deprivation and the pain of our nation's first people. I knew it would change the negative view so widely held about the Aboriginal community, and could create a very different dynamic about how we see ourselves as a people. Our history of links to Britain, our allegiance to the Allied powers, our status in the Asia-Pacific region, our multicultural pride and our easygoing personality are floating elements of the whole—but we miss the glue of ancient heritage that could better ground us, pull us all together into our own unique identity. We reject it. John and I continued to believe, in some small way, we could build a bridge for others to enter the magical spirit of place that is the culture of Aboriginal Australia, and so open up the possibility of more open exchange. It would be a dialogue about community, respect for place, and celebration of the human spirit.

A few small design jobs began coming our way after Budget Rent-a-Car, owned at the time by the entrepreneur Bob Ansett and his wife Josie, hired us to create textiles for their new corporate wardrobe. The Budget job had made us a little money, but it was the belief the Ansetts had in us and our ideas that mattered most. It was the first breakthrough in our quest to signature Australia in a different way. We now had a major Australian corporation willing to wear our designs proudly. We still look back at that shiny, slick Budget catalogue and marvel with gratitude that the Ansetts had the faith to go with us when no-one else would. A little later Nexus, a prominent Melbourne interior design company, invited us to pitch for a carpet for a public building in the Snowy Mountains, and we were stunned when our concept won the commission.

We regained some confidence, too, to look again at making retail products. We needed to find an ongoing commercial engine to stabilise our income. We'd had our fingers burned by product at the very start, when we made a wildly inaccurate guess about the volume of stock we might sell in The Hague on our exhibiting trip in 1983. We ended up with $50,000 worth of scarves sitting idle in our garage, creating a financial noose around our necks, and taking most of my time on the phone or on the streets trying to sell them. Generally our sales pitches were in vain. There was no interest from shops anywhere in Australia in anything Indigenous.

On one occasion I was in the middle of a presentation to buyers at David Jones in Adelaide when—after they'd left us standing by the entrance for almost an hour—Tim vomited orange juice all over their pale pink carpet. If they'd been reluctant to see me before Tim's unfortunate mishap, they understandably ejected us after it. Usually, I didn't make it to the meeting stage at all. My introduction on the phone generally was cut short with a 'Sorry, we're not doing brown this year'. It was only when I could jam my foot in the door somehow, and keep it there long enough to present our products with their strong, simple designs in a kaleidoscope of landscape colours, that attitudes began to change.

An exception was Qantas, who'd featured our first collection of silk and wool scarves in their in-flight shopping catalogue soon after our 1983 launch. We couldn't have known that Balarinji's pathway would lead to Qantas on a number of defining future occasions, but our first small collaboration was already an extension of the emotion we always felt when we saw the white kangaroo on a red aircraft tail on foreign tarmacs. It was a bubbling up of pride in being Australian, and it was similar to the feeling that washed over me when I sat by the campfire with

John's relations at Borroloola and felt the warmth of being with family in the bush.

We took a leap of faith in 1987. We moved our design tables out of the side room of our St Peters house, and rented two small offices on the outskirts of the Adelaide CBD. The move ended up prolonging the time it would take before we achieved financial stability, but it started to feel like a real business. I would sometimes sit in my bare office there, looking around for a few minutes, hearing our (very part-time) secretary answer the phone with our company name, just soaking up the excitement of having a base outside home. But frequent calls from our nervous bankers kept our noses to the grindstone and our feet on the ground.

We began to get some traction with licensing designs to manufacturers for fashion accessories, tableware, umbrellas and clothing. It was a slow drip-feed to building a merchandise business, as it was based on receiving a small percentage of each item sold. But it allowed us to forget about making, warehousing and selling products. That could be left to the experts. Instead, we could concentrate on our mission—to blend ancient designs with a contemporary world to speak truthfully and respectfully about Aboriginal culture and its place in Australia's view of itself.

We shared the building with an obstetrician, which was a handy coincidence when I fell pregnant in April 1988—I just needed to pop across the corridor for my monthly checks. I'd miscarried the year before, so we were nervous. But all went smoothly, and our daughter Julia was born three weeks early in December. She was a truly beautiful baby. Her generous heart shone from when she was tiny, and she exuded a calm acceptance of the constant eruption of our life around her. She was a Bicentennial baby—born two hundred years after Captain Cook brought the Anglo-Saxon side of her ancestry to Australian shores.

And she was born just in time to be the centrepiece of the holy family—us—in the church nativity play. The congregation who'd witnessed our boys' high spirits most Sundays of the year would have scarcely recognised their angelic faces in the nave. It was a happier occasion than John remembered as a childhood shepherd in the boys' home, where he'd tried in vain to both kneel and keep the soles of his shoes, full of holes, firmly on the floor.

The arrival of our third child coincided with John deciding he could no longer be party to the sham that was Aboriginal affairs in South Australia; he quit his job to start a consultancy. The safety net was gone, we had a business that had still not yielded us a salary, and somehow we needed to feed and house ourselves, our boys and a baby girl. I recall a mate of John offering advice on his deliberations to throw in his job. In an interesting twist to the deep-end theory, he said John would feel he was diving from the platform, but really he was just slipping in from the side. I wasn't sure we were swimming in the same pool as this guy, as I felt the outlook was bleak.

Two pieces of luck saved us. One was that the 1996 Melbourne Olympic Bid signed John up for eighteen months to help them lobby Africa. A few years earlier, he'd chaired the Second World Black and African Festival of Arts and Culture for the Asia-Pacific zone, and later coordinated Nigeria for the Melbourne congress of the Commonwealth Heads of Government Meeting—CHOGM. His network of African contacts was a ready resource for Melbourne, as was the fact he'd been an elite black athlete—the first Indigenous player to be selected to play soccer for Australia. The second lifeline was that Merle Griffin, the elderly woman who had taken John's only baby photos, gave us $10,000 to put in an account for groceries. John's income helped service our business debt, and Merle's incredible gift fed us all for more than a year. It gave us the breathing space we so desperately needed.

With John away a lot of the time in Nigeria, Ivory Coast and Congo, the next two years were a constant juggling act for us both as we strove to look after three children and keep the business from going to the wall. The design studio continued to be high risk, but the success we were beginning to see in our licensed branded products meant we could hire more support and design staff. We recruited a studio team from both Indigenous and non-Indigenous backgrounds. It was a deliberate strategy to open up pathways for a mix of artists and designers to work with us towards a new, original graphic statement about Australia. With John's ever-vigilant eye on protocols and integrity, we began to push the boundaries of where our ideas could take us.

We always discussed the business openly around the dinner table. It was a good hedge to questions about the expensive toys and gadgets that many of the children's friends' families could more easily afford. Tim was still very young, ten or eleven, but in response to my complaints yet another night about impossible cash flow, he said we were building the base of a pyramid. Using his hands to illustrate the correlation between the width of a base and the height of an apex, he said the more effort and money we put into the base the bigger it would be, and the taller the pyramid we'd be able to grow. That picture has come to mind many times over the years since, when progress has been slow or investment in opportunities has been seemingly wasted. It has been a caution against compromise. It was also a handy reply to Tim in years to come when he would start his own business, and financial stress would mean surviving for weeks on boiled carrots and penniless zeal. While we would never have let him drown, the realities of entrepreneurial hardship taught him more than an eager safety net from his parents could have.

John and I had made a pact very early on in the business that the children would come first, no matter what, as at the end of the day they, and their generation, were the reason we were doing all this. So we spent every spare minute we had with them. Tim, James and Julia enjoyed childhoods full of flute, violin and cello lessons, soccer clubs, big gatherings of family and friends, and camping trips all over the state and the country. They screamed down massive sand dunes at South Australia's Coffin Bay, launching themselves like missiles into deepest, bluest water. Mucking around in a boat in crystal-clear bays kept them amused for hours. We snorkelled in and out of the inlets of Yorke Peninsula for abalone and crays. We drove for days on end to the steamy top of Queensland, took Christmas flights to visit family in Tasmania and walk the mountains in falling summer snow. And as often as we could, we drove the five long days north to the Gulf. Julia loved it as much as her brothers, rolling out her swag, fishing by the river and eating from the coals. Not one of them was ever keen to leave the carefree life in the bush behind when it came time to head south once more.

They learned many of the lessons of the bush from John on those trips, some not so palatable. Camping on the beach in the far west of South Australia, we'd watched a wide-winged skate glide up and down the shoreline for almost a week. The children had leaned out of their tin dinghy to talk to it, rowing quietly in its wake. On the sixth day our meat had gone bad in the esky, so John speared the skate, shredded and rinsed its flesh in the seawater, and threw it on the coals. The children gagged, and ate biscuits in preference to their mate. John and I ate a lot of skate that night to impress on the children that if you kill it, you eat it.

Our freezer in the garage in Adelaide was quite an attraction for our children's friends, with its occasional contents of echidna, turtle, wombat or dugong. We ran foul of the German press at one point, taking a batch of sea turtle eggs to a meet-and-greet night at a prominent city restaurant. The white of sea turtle eggs doesn't coagulate when cooked, and they arrived, runny, at the table for sampling. I thought the journalists' reticence was due to the look of the eggs, but it turned out their pursed lips were in fury that we'd harvested them. John tried to explain that they'd come from family by road and by air from the Gulf via Darwin, with the hope of keeping John in touch with his traditional lands.

By 1991 John's tenure with the Melbourne Olympic Bid was over, and the design business needed to step up to centre stage. We were on a merry-go-round we couldn't step off, and there was no Plan B. A pivotal breakthrough came early that year, when one of Japan's largest textile mills, Nittobo, sought us out to create a licensed womenswear collection for the giant Japanese fashion label Kashyama Onward. A young Melbourne girl, Kim Chadwick, on an internship at Nittobo, had suggested they create an Australian Indigenous concept. Balarinji was on a list the trade commission had put together for Kim, and she came to Adelaide with Nittobo executives to see our work. We all hit it off immediately, and after a return visit to Japan and several hours in a Tokyo boardroom, contracts were signed. People talk about their discomfort with silences in Japanese negotiations. Aboriginal people, however, are masters of silence, and we had plenty of practice in patience to bring to the table.

The deadlines Nittobo set were almost impossible, and over the last three days of completing the collection we slept a total of six hours. Our staff didn't sleep much more. Sinking into bed after the courier had picked up our paintings was like falling comatose into an endless, happy chasm. We knew we'd done absolutely all we could to make the most of the opportunity. Just weeks later, our designs were in production. We watched at the mill in Osaka while our textiles cascaded from the print tables in a riot of saturated Australian colours, astounded by the fact that fabrics by Yves Saint Laurent were spilling out from the next conveyor belt over. The Balarinji range of colourful dresses, shirts and skirts took pride of place alongside brands like Comme des Garçons and Issey Miyake on the designer floor at one of Japan's largest department stores, Isetan, at Shinjuku, Tokyo's famous shopping district. I pinched myself standing next to John with three dozen long-stemmed pale pink roses in my arms, presented to us in celebration of our opening. It seemed a long way from waiting for an hour to be rejected by buyers at David Jones in Adelaide.

Swimwear followed our fashion ranges in Japan, as well as delicately woven silk kimonos, cotton yukata house coats, bindings for tatami matting for the floors of houses, microfibre eyewear cloths, pyjamas, underwear, surfwear and prints on paper. The business we wrote was exciting, but Japan's fascination with the themes we were presenting was the real buzz. Their media wanted to know about the ancient culture that underpinned our work. They drew parallels with the ancient traditions of Japan, where respect for customs and for elders still largely permeated modern family life. They were enthralled that Aboriginal culture pre-dated the famous prehistoric cave art of Lascaux in France and the pyramids of Egypt by tens of thousands of years. The songlines we described of land and spirits that carved a path across country resonated with the Japanese religion of Shinto, and its beliefs about animism. The questions were insightful and far reaching.

There was an almost reverential response to aspects of the interface. One visit we took boomerangs as gifts for associate companies. At the reception where we presented them, Nittobo executive Hidenari Shibuya came up to us, concerned. We had embarrassed the president of one of our licensees with the magnitude of the gift. I hastened to explain that while these boomerangs were certainly real, and well carved and engraved, they were not an expensive item. But my protests went unheeded, and a gift to reciprocate the treasure we'd given came back. An exquisite handmade, fine-rimmed ceramic bowl, shallow and imperfectly round, inlaid with squares of 24 carat gold.

Like so many Australian endeavours, we were generating far greater respect and interest away from home, but our success in Japan did spark renewed focus on us in Australia. When Mr Shibuya took us to meet his school friend, the senior monk of the famous Kiyomizu Temple in Kyoto, Film Australia was there to record the exchange for a documentary about our work. We hoped the attention would progress our goals at home.

We learned a great deal about the expression of culture in Japan. Mr Shibuya was an enigmatic person in the well-rounded Japanese tradition. His day job at Nittobo was just one aspect of a diverse life. A potter, gardener, poet and martial arts exponent, Mr Shibuya approached business in a particularly Japanese way. John and I sat with him on wooden walkways overlooking the white-pebbled calm of Zen gardens. We dined on regional delicacies in Tokyo, Kyoto and Osaka, in tiny upstairs eating houses with their indigo-curtained alcoves, and skin-fine porcelain bowls. The wonder of golden pavilions in carp-filled lakes, of camellia and begonia gardens spilling over rope-trussed fences, and the solemn solidity of Shogun fortresses melded commerce with aesthetics in a wholly satisfying way. It taught us much about taking the time to savour the many dimensions of interaction within a business relationship, and not to underestimate the personal rewards that ensue regardless of monetary success—and that building relationships of personal trust are more likely to bring financial results. John saw great affinity with the way Aboriginal people do 'business'; taking the time to know someone is always the precursor to other matters.

The Japanese approach to art and design also nourished our creative approach. We soaked up their spare aesthetic, their ability to distil an idea to its essence, and their devotion to the handmade form. Subtle tone on tone, clear stark colour, and juxtaposition of natural materials like wood, stone and cotton created a clever harmony across public spaces, cultural institutions, things to buy and places to eat. Their approach transcended the manmade, and encompassed nature that we saw around us—the fleeting ethereal beauty of sakura blossoms before they fell, the carefully trained branches of bonsai, and the steamy bathing waters of volcanic onsen. The 'Japanese experience', on the surface at least, was so readily defined and accessed. I didn't doubt that complexities lay underneath in the changing tastes of the younger generation and the tensions all cultures experience in the process of modernisation. There was such a strength, though, in the self-confidence and self-knowledge that seemed to come from their wealth of tradition. And a unity in their community from their willingness to acknowledge the power of their culture, and include its ancient rhythms in their daily lives.

Mr Shibuya and his collegue, Tadashi Yamamoto, visited us in Australia too. John took them to Uluru, and they said the spiritual aura of the Rock was a physical sensation. They came in order to better understand the ethos of our work. What it meant and what was driving it. We were still speaking largely to deaf ears in Australia, where the market could accept tourist trinkets but saw no place for an absorption of Indigenous themes into the images and objects that we see and use every day. The cottagy flowers of Britain, the slick minimalism of Scandinavia and the indistinguishable international lines of most things in between defined, or failed to define, an 'Australian' image.

Yet we could see that John's family had a desire to share their culture with other Australians, to see it valued. It was remarkable, in the light of dispossession. Annie's view that Australia is big enough for *every*one, ringing out across the ceremony camp, is an extremely generous position in view of the history of the Yanyuwa. Annie often commented that she didn't know how the breakdown began. Why people came to live in Borroloola rather than stay in the islands or on the river, where life was better. She talked about welfare and whitefellas just 'coming over people'.

I wondered, on all those visits back to the Gulf over the years, how things had become so bad. I knew the basic facts—life in the bush had been superseded by life in town, with the resulting deterioration of active, healthy lifestyles, and loss of traditional ceremonial life. I'd seen the social repercussions in field trips to many parts of Australia with my departmental job. But the endemic poverty and squalor that was getting worse every time we returned to Borroloola? Clearly the chain of events that had snowballed to an intractable conclusion had started with the empire-swelling colonists and officials rounding everyone up to live in town. Aboriginal land would have been vacated for white expansion, and it would have been easier to administer services and channel black kids into European schools. However, while there is some truth to that sequence of events there was not widespread forcible 'rounding up' of people, and it is a simplistic account of what actually happened. Annie's view of the changes simply 'coming over people' is a more accurate reflection on how the debilitating, irreversible dependency that is the lifelong reality for so many Aboriginal people simply crept up on them.

There is ample documentation by early government officials, long-term field workers, teachers, Borroloola residents, and pre-eminent anthropologists, linguists, historians and geographers in books, theses, films, field notes and audio recordings of how the history of the Yanyuwa played out, and what the repercussions have been. Government records from the earliest days of contact tell one side of the picture and are naturally flawed by their times and their agenda of legitimising dispossession and its accompanying violence.

Focus on Borroloola by a number of academics from the 1960s onwards changed the bias, and Yanyuwa were given a mouthpiece to tell their own version of events. It is a fascinating journey of discovery for those who want to know how a group of Aboriginal people interpret their own past, present and future. Access to these insights has been facilitated by a stream of highly credible researchers and collaborators who have put their hearts and much of their lives into this work. Most prominent among them have been linguists John Bradley and the late Jean F. Kirton, anthropologist John Avery, geographer Richard Baker, and the late Alice Moyle, an ethnomusicologist. To know the Yanyuwa is to enter a world of humbling generosity, and the revelationary work of these and others reflects the intimacy and reciprocity of the relationships. It is principally from their work that I have supplemented the stories I have heard from John and from wider Yanyuwa family themselves, to relate something of the riches of Yanyuwa ceremonial life and the history of contact that backdrops the tumultuous times of the last generation of full Yanyuwa Law women.

Observations of Yanyuwa living tribally were noted by explorer Matthew Flinders as he sailed the northern coasts of Australia between 1802 and 1803. He named the Yanyuwa's island homelands the Sir Edward Pellew Group, after an officer in the British navy. His party described 'Indians' travelling in bark canoes, and commented on the remains of many fires where turtle had been cooked. And the Yanyuwa noted *him* too. Annie remembered the stories her family passed down. *Matthew Plinders* (sic) *came round there before. Where the Macassan used to be before. After Macassan. Because I heard the words they used to telling me, all my people used to telling me. Matthew Plinders, he just went past. And he saw the people there walking around with the cock rag. Ha ha. Like napkin. No clothes on. Yeah.*

A cairn in cement on Observation Island marks Flinders's visit: *Erected in memory of Commander Matthew Flinders, Royal Navy, HMS Investigator, December 1802.* On the south-east point of the land he named Centre Island, he stopped at a rocky hillock, oblivious to the Yanyuwa sacred site he stood on. Two boys of the Dreaming had a bush oven there and tried to cook bats in it. But the bats were friends of the Rainbow Serpent, and every time the boys lifted the lid they were not cooked and flew out.

German expeditionist Ludwig Leichhardt crossed the McArthur River near its tidal limits in 1845, close to the future site of the Borroloola township. Musso remembered the story that family told him about Leichhardt. People said he came west from Queensland and headed towards the north-west and up towards Arnhem Land. They could smell him before they could see him. Leichhardt noted he was following existing Aboriginal pathways, enabling him to cross the McArthur at a safe distance from the river's crocodile-infested estuary downstream, and its deep sandstone gorges upstream. Leichhardt and his party disappeared on an ill-fated second expedition in 1848, and no trace was ever found of them. Rumours that a German-speaking man living with

111

'McArthur river blacks' was Leichhardt's brother-in-law, Classen, were never substantiated, but it is a plausible story. The man was shot during a punitive raid. The route that Leichhardt followed became the road that tourists drive on today.

By the early 1900s families like Annie's were still living in the bush, commuting between their islands and the mainland at will, while further south Aboriginal tribes were engaged in bloody collision with the colonists. Annie's memories of her bush childhood are of a life lived according to a different paradigm from the one she would soon encounter.

I been grow up islands, no whitefellas around. I was born Vanderlin Island—called Wardi. I am Jungkayi *for this island—caretaker for country and ceremony on mother's side—because my uncle and my grandfather country and my mother country. When I was a tiny little girl, I used to running around in the beach, at the island, Centre Island, everywhere, South West too, called Warnarrwarnarr, because my father was from South West, and grandfather. I am* Ngimarringki *for that country—boss on father's side. And my mother, she's from Centre Island, North Island. We call that place Barranyi. Barranyi from North Island, Centre Island, all them country. This is the way we call them. Really way. Our mother country. My grandfather country. My great-grandfather. Centre Island. My spirit coming back to my land because all our grandfather's country. My* mimi, *my mother's father.*

My grandmother married Garrawa people. She was a Garrawa woman, and she got all the children for her from the Centre Island, from North Island, that place for us now.

Little girl, you know. We used to stay, not stay in one place, but we used to go place to place. Yeah. Come back here for tobacca. My father, mother, used to come back for tobacca. To Borroloola. And go back to the island, sleeping around, we used to live sometime at Manangoora

112

too. Travelling around with the canoe. Around South West Island, Centre Island. Our father used to go hunting, because we used to starve. No food. Not long ago we got this whitefella's tucker, not long ago. Living on turtle. Fish. Stingray. Sugarbag. And dugong too, big feed. That's the way we been grown up with that feast.

People had ceremonies. Song about A-kuridi—groper. They used to make a log coffin. Sing that A-kuridi song when they were making log coffin for people who died. The spirit when someone dies goes back to the place and there is the spirit inside in them in the rock. Painting on the rock. It is a spirit. A-kuridi, the groper, put the people from the Dreamtime in there. All the Jungkayi people, and Ngimarringki for this country have to look after those paintings.

Make rope from wattle trees. Skin him that bark to get rope out of the tree. Twist it around. Inside part is lovely for make a rope. Who put that rope tree there—that Dreaming now. That's A-kuridi. Everything she leave. Everything she left over here. The big rock, and call the name of place, country, the islands. Put the rope on the harpoon for hunting dugong.

Sea eagle, that's my mother. Because sea eagle got big Dreaming and ceremony. When my people die, he come around and cackle around and 'ha, kwak' keep calling. The bird and the stone Dreaming—A-kuwaykuwayk—its power is around country. You can hear it in the night, but you can't see it. He sings he is holding up the sky. Not falling down. Because that's the Law from Aboriginal people, from my grandfather and my uncles. That's the story they used to tell us.

People get their mark, their design, for ceremony from their mother, or their father side, or grandfather. Might be the white eagle-hawk, A-karnkarnka, or the dugong killer—their mob called Li-maramaranja people.

Jungkayi can't just pass through country. Look around for

everything. We stop for a while, fishing and hunting around in the sea. Camping.

You can't swear where bujimala—Rainbow Serpent—*might drown you. And don't call the name* bujimala *when you are travelling in the sea. That's my uncle Tim and my father. On sacred islands, you can't kill snake or lizard or anything. That's mean that wind might come, you know, like a cyclone and all that.*

No sugarbag around here Centre Island, nothing. This is the Law. The kuwaykuwayk—*the wayku sorcery stone*—*put this Law and you can't bring your sugarbag into this island now. It's the Law. You can't break the Law. This is only the* Yijan, *our Dreaming. But bee coming*—*coming to this island and get all the flowers to make a sugarbag honey on South West Island.*

Take the leaf off the mijirr *tree. And boil them up. Use it for where we are sick, hot, something like that, headache, and sometimes for eyes too.*

We used to collect in the bush, make leaf wine. We used to pick it up. Called mararangai.

Grandfather used to get a vine called ma-murnda. *Eat the roots. Sometime we get for something like a dugong, leaf, and make a bed then. In the oven*—*ground oven. And cook them up (the roots, on the fire). They good, like a potato, something like that. I can tell this, because my grandmother used to get them. And they used to teach us to eat them.*

Ma-mundarrarra, *like a seed . . . something like beans, like that. Cook them, and get it out from fire and eat him up.*

We never used to see money like, you know, now. Like flour, no sugar, no tea-leaf anywhere. We used to get sugarbag, honey. Cutting in the tree. Just water we drink. Sugarbag with hot water. We never see any sugar or milk or something like that. Early in the morning we used to get up. Walk around, go hunting again, look for sugarbag once again. Sometimes for fish. Good one, crab. I like the claw.

You can see them islands all in the song. In Yanyuwa song. All about country. I'm singer, I'm dancer. I don't know why they (young people) can't sing. We teach them. Old ladies died now, taught us how to sing our islands, on everything in the sea.

Annie's words lament the passing of the songs of the land: the death of the generation that handed them to her, and the broken chain of young people able to sing them. Yet her Dreamings remain undiluted in her life. Their power is undiminished.

6

Compassion

ngarramilmila
My chest is warm when I have compassion.

When I have compassion for you, my heart feels good.
When I show you my emotion I know the warmth
of being brave.

Day 6, Wednesday 31 May 2006

a nnie is tired. One of the women calls to her. 'Good morning, *Kukurdi*.' Annie sleeps on. She tells me she was born in 1930, which makes her seventy-six. It is a long, arduous trip for a seventy-six-year-old. And her responsibilities here are emotionally heavy. She sits up as the sky begins to lighten a little more. The evening star is hanging, and the other stars are still there, but dimming. The Milky Way has faded into day.

'We have sadness, yes, sadness,' says Annie. A song in language.

'Good morning, Yuwani,' she says as she sees me stir in my swag next to her. 'Did you have a good sleep, my dear?'

We sit around the fire at breakfast. Anticipation is building. Today is dancing day. Songs and dance movements are practised. Headbands are tried on, adjusted. There is last-minute sewing of elastic into newly hemmed dancing skirts. The song women practise to beating sticks. Carefully assembled feathers are retrieved from bags where they have been stored for the moment when the ceremony begins. A card game continues during the wait. Tears of grief surface in quiet moments.

But it is mostly laughter that permeates this sisterhood without a cause. Feminism would be unfathomable here. Unnecessary. There is no tyranny between the sexes. Just deep respect and a valued respective place in the world. Expressed with the reassurance of generations of the Law. There is no guesswork. The rules of relationships are enshrined in lifelong teaching and example, handed down through the ages. The men guess about women's secrets, and the women guess about the men's, but they respect each other's Dreamings.

Annie's sense of humour is sharp. Her granddaughter from the city has a large ring on her finger.

'You got husband?' Annie asks her.

'No,' Samantha replies, 'they all scared of me, eh. This ring amber. Sap that's in the earth for a million years.'

'You millionaire?' Annie quips.

The women start to dress. White ochre is mixed with oil. There is a rush now. Hurry up. One of my nieces, Kathakatha Isa McDinny, tells me I will be dancing.

'No,' Baba Thelma says. 'Tomorrow. Tonight you can practise.'

I am co-opted to apply thick white ochre to soft black skin warmed by the mid-morning sun. Sacred patterns from the Dreaming. I copy the images from the line of women already painted. Thelma asks me to get some charcoal from the fire to add to the patterning. 'Not a burning piece,' she grins.

They wait at the edge of the campsite to be called. I go out with Annie, the song woman, the ceremony boss, to sit on the edge of the dancing space on the ceremony ground. She taps the ground by her left hip to tell me where to sit. We watch other tribes already dancing.

'Strong Dreamin',' Annie whispers.

Finally the Borroloola women dance. Proud and true. I feel a sense of pride and belonging that I have done nothing to deserve. They know their culture, their ceremonies. They are strong from the secrets they know. From the secrets they don't tell. Tragically, from the secrets that will die with them. Annie's singing rings out across the circle.

John's mother, Kathleen Murrmayibinya, and nursing sister, Ruth Heathcock, McArthur River, around 1940. *Photo*: Miss E.M. Griffin, John Moriarty Collection, National Museum of Australia.

John, aged two, at Donergan's Camp, McArthur River, Borroloola, around 1940. *Photo:* Miss E.M. Griffin, John Moriarty Collection, National Museum of Australia.

Donergan in dugout canoe, McArthur River, around 1940. *Photo*: Miss E.M. Griffin, John Moriarty Collection, National Museum of Australia.

Baby Tim, aged fifteen months, during his naming time, with Old Tim Rakuwurlma, Borroloola, 1982. *Photo:* John Moriarty.

Tim and James, Balarinji bed linen for Sheridan, 1985. *Photo*: Adelaide Advertiser.

Ros in Central Australia mixing colours,1986. *Photo*: John Moriarty.

Julia's Christening, Adelaide, 1989. Left to right: Julia, Ros, James (aged five), Tim (aged seven) and John.

James, Tim and Julia holding an echidna, Tasmania, 1993. *Photo*: John Moriarty.

Ros and John, Sydney Airport, Wunala Dreaming, 2004. *Photo*: Garry Saunders.

Sunset, Borroloola, 2006. *Photo:* Tim Moriarty.

John with Thelma Douglas Walwalmara, The Crossing, McArthur River, Borroloola, 2006. *Photo:* Ros Moriarty.

Annie Isaac Karrakayn, The Crossing, McArthur River, Borroloola, 2006. *Photo:* Ros Moriarty.

Ceremony Week, first night transit camp at a railway siding of the main north-south line from Darwin to Adelaide, 2006. *Photo:* Ros Moriarty.

Isa McDinny a-Yubuya, Ceremony Week transit camp, 2006. *Photo:* Ros Moriarty.

Rosie Noble a-Makandurnamara, Borroloola ceremony ground, 2006.
Photo: Ros Moriarty.

Left to right: Thelma Dixon Kuniburinya, Isa McDinny a-Yubuya, Edna Pluto a- Maliyawuna, Linda McDinny a-Wambadurna, Rosie Noble a-Makandurnamara, at transit camp, 2006. *Photo:* Ros Moriarty.

Thelma Douglas Walwalmara, Ceremony Week transit camp, 2006. *Photo:* Ros Moriarty.

Linda McDinny a-Wambadurna and Edna Pluto a-Maliyawuna, Ceremony Week transit camp, 2006. *Photo:* Ros Moriarty.

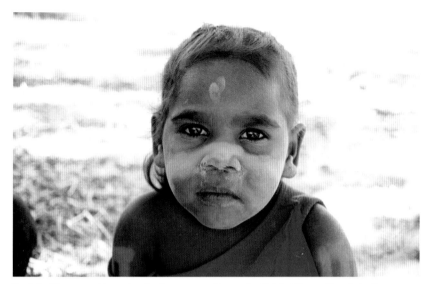

Laticia Norman, Borroloola Ceremony Ground, 2006. *Photo:* Ros Moriarty.

Caroline Rory, Ceremony Week transit camp, 2006. *Photo:* Ros Moriarty.

Nancy McDinny a-Yukuwalmara, Ros Moriarty, Isa McDinny a-Yubuya, transit camp on return from Ceremony Week, 2006.

Isa McDinny a-Yubuya at Centre Island handback ceremony, 2007. *Photo:* John Moriarty.

Flying over Glyde River, Yanyuwa country, the land that John was ripped away from, 2006. *Photo:* John Moriarty.

Annie Isaac Karrakayn at
Centre Island handback
ceremony, 2007.
Photo: John Moriarty.

Jemima Miller Wuwarlu with her daughter Joanna Miller and granddaughter
Rosella Miller, at the Yanyuwa town camp, Borroloola, 2007. *Photo:* Ros
Moriarty.

Fire tree on John's mother country, Wardawadala, 2008. *Photo:* John Moriarty.

Nancy McDinny
a-Yukuwalmara digging for
turtle, Wardawadala, 2008.
Photo: Ros Moriarty.

Rachael McDinny a-Mulyurrkulmanya hunting at Wardawadala, 2008.
Photo: Ros Moriarty.

Afterwards, lines of women approach the Borroloola women, seated up front now around Yuwani Annie. The exchange is more than communal. It is communion. It is profoundly moving. I find my eyes filling with tears yet again, with the power of the human connection. As the other women approach, Annie gestures to me and says, 'Say hello to my daughter-in-law, this is my daughter-in-law.'

I wonder to myself if the situation were reversed, and a black woman from the bush turned up at a comparable occasion of pomp and tradition—maybe the coronation of the King of England—and dressed differently, didn't know the protocols, made cultural mistakes, would the audience show the same tolerance towards her as has been shown to me this week? Particularly by this bush queen, my mother-in-law, the ceremony boss entrusted with forty thousand years of precious and irreplaceable knowledge.

Here in the desert, the ceremony is central. But the card playing, relaxing on swags, laughing, talking, reminding each other of stories—it is all time out for women who are easy in each other's company. There is ritualised gifting and receiving. Sharing. It's the Law.

In the dusk, they teach me to dance. Isa, one of my Kathakathas, one of the best dancers, tells me to take my shoes off. Nothing cultural—'You might trip.' She shows me where to place my feet, how to rhythmically bring my knees together, at the same time following a counter pattern with my arms and hands. Looks so simple. Hard to do in repetition. Isa and the others clap in encouragement at my feeble attempts. When I get a couple of moves half right, my teacher Kathakatha hugs me, presses her face on mine. 'Borroloola winner!' she laughs.

The sunset sky is layered sponge cake again. Blue on the

horizon and pink above. 'Cold night,' they all tell me. The old people always knew: 'This sky, cold night.'

There is night dancing on the ceremony ground. We sit in close rings around fires to try to keep warm. It is cold.

Yuwani Annie is up in the night. Her body is racked with her coughing. I find my torch as she hunts through her bag for chest rub. She has a tablet box for daily blood pressure pills, eye drops and cough medicine. She is sick. She shows me a large lump that has come up in her leg again. Whenever I ask her if she's okay, she tells me, 'Yeah, I'm all right.' The support team sent nurses around the camps yesterday. Everyone has blood pressure problems. It's not much of a step to stroke, heart disease and kidney failure.

I lie on my back in my swag, drinking in the night sky above me, while Annie settles back to sleep. They have told me I will be dancing out on the ceremony ground tomorrow. It was a scary thought before. Now it is petrifying. There is a lyricism, grace, about the Borroloola dancers that seems singular among the groups here. Their songs have a melodic quality that stays in your head. The modulations form an imprint on your mind. The beat of sticks and hands resonates in your ears. Technical proficiency allows a form and shape to the choreography that seems spontaneous. But it is neither arbitrary nor accidental. It has a pattern that is entirely deliberate: torsos leaning towards and away from each other, shifting arms and expressive hands. The addition of a white learner in full view on the ceremony ground will surely diminish this purity. But I am learning that the women of my Borroloola family are less concerned with perfection than with inclusion. '*Kina palirra*. Thank you. You are there.'

Compassion

∞

I OFTEN THOUGHT ABOUT the fact that my background and John's represented two vastly different sides of our country. My own forebears had gravitated to Australia in convict ships and by free passage; they had preached in Methodist churches and run drinking houses; they'd raised families of well-dressed children on country estates; bought houses and land and businesses for their future prosperity; had jobs in factories and shops. They'd made their own destiny. In the same two centuries, John's forebears had been buried alive, coerced from their lands, hunted and shot, humiliated by white masters and left to rot in squalid outback town camps. They'd had their destiny stolen from them. How could such histories be part of one proud Australian story?

While these were things I'd learned from listening and reading, they were the reality of John's living family story. And of many, many Aboriginal people like him. Not an anonymous account of colonial settlement in Australia from a tome on a library shelf.

On our many trips to Borroloola, the continuing deep injustice of the Aboriginal situation in modern Australia was on full display. History can sometimes be forgiven—enlightenment can be hidden under the shroud of its era. Its disastrous ongoing consequences cannot, however, in the face of national prosperity and capacity be ignored. On the ground in Borroloola, the inertia of the solutions made my skin crawl. John's family's patient acceptance of what life had delivered made the sadness tragic. That people refused to be destroyed was an inspiration.

People had tried hard to keep their community strong when change began to 'come over' Yanyuwa families like Annie's. By 1910, police arriving in Borroloola to control lawless whites started handing out rations to elderly and infirm Aboriginal people. Many older Yanyuwa who had been living in the bush were coming in for flour, sugar, tea and tobacco. Ceremony was still paramount, and in an inventive assimilation of new ways flour was mixed with water and used for body paint as an alternative to travelling to ochre pits to excavate white pigment.

Malandarri camp, on the other side of the McArthur River from the Borroloola township, was home to people living between town and the bush. The Yanyuwa had always intended it to be temporary, just another beautiful seasonal camping place by fresh water, where tucker was more plentiful in times of scarcity. People were still going out to their traditional lands to hunt, for ceremony and for family gatherings, and coming back in on ration day. Babies, including John, were still being born bush way at the birthing camp on the riverbank. Baba Thelma remembers the magical songs that took away the pain of childbirth.

The old people, you know, women, had a song. When the woman never delivered a baby quickly, they had the song, and they used to rub a stone behind their back. And then they used to deliver the baby straight away. No pain.

Dinah remembers the birthing place too.

Been have my children along bush. Along Malandarri. My mother been the nurse. Before that, for big fella my son, my husband been nurse. Yeah. True. I been have 'im along bush. Been come quick.

Malandarri was not a bush camp and not a town camp either. It was a halfway place, where people erected dwellings under the savannah canopy, from paperbark, flattened kerosene tins and timber posts. It was central in the lives of the women of Annie's vintage and a little older and a little younger, who grew up between the islands, Manangoora salt works on the Wearyan and this camp. There was no evidence left of Malandarri by the time we were visiting from the 1980s on, but the vivid stories of it were very much alive.

Yuwani Dinah's father was a boss at Malandarri, and was consequently nicknamed 'Government'. The quasi town life that he 'governed' did not at first diminish the ways of the bush, and clan hierarchies and cultural teaching were still important in Malandarri life, even though European settlement was just a stone's throw away.

As a child, Dinah would go down to the river from Malandarri.

Go down along river. Swim. My mum used to sing out, Don't swim there. Look out for crocodile there.

'Nah, nothing. I gotta swim. I like river.'

I used to go hunting. I used to go along my mum. Used to show me for bream, goanna, for blue-tongue. Cut 'im sugarbag. Used to cry too, you know.

'I need sugarbag.'

'Nah, leave 'im for camp.'

'Nah, I'm hungry.'

Must be born along island. I dunno. (The others tell me Dinah's mother gave birth to her in a dugout canoe between the island and the mainland. Said they made fire for cooking in the canoe too.) *School along bush for ceremony. Used to dance for me. My mother used to dance. For ceremony. For tell me that big ceremony. She been learn me, my mum. And for public corroboree. For dance. Yeah, used to learn me.*

'You got to dance, you got to learn, you got to carry on ceremony and public dance. You got to carry on dance before I die. Mmmm.'

Used to paint 'im.

We used to walk from Manangoora right up to Borroloola. Long way. Camp two night, halfway. Used to carry 'im little bit of a swag. I used to carry mine, when I been little one.

Jemima Miller Wuwarlu moved into Malandarri to live with her aunty and grandmother.

We been moved from Manangoora right up to Borroloola. Old people used to get ration here, welfare time. But I liked living along bush. Better for me. Go hunting for goanna, or turtle or blue-tongue. Sugarbag. Lily, we eat. Quiet. And happy too. Happy along bush, because we been learn from little tiny. Our parents been teach us.

But my uncle didn't have kids. My aunty, and my grandfather my mimi, and my grandmother old lady, I used to stay with them. My mother been in Manangoora. But I used to stay with my aunty and uncle across at Malandarri.

During the years that Malandarri remained a temporary camp, ceremony continued in the bush on the mainland and on the islands. The young men's ceremony—the a-Marndiwa ceremony, boys' initiation—was among the most important, and there are locations where it is still continued today. It is important for holding the country.

Very strict, Thelma says. *You don't have to talk about with men. Because that women business. Men have business too. Men business. We don't ask. We know where they're going. And they don't ask us, they know where we're going.*

At ceremony time, for big ceremony, we get together, stay together, and we go up to the ceremony ground together. All right. We sing for them and they dance. The ladies dance. We don't see the man when they're dancing up top too. This is very important for us. When they finish up there, we finish down here. Nothing. They don't watch woman ceremony. The ladies dance all night. And then we finish in the morning. Go back home, and the parents belong to the young people, they cook for us. And then the men gonna come down, and they gonna do the dance all night again. They dance all night, and then, maybe early in the morning, like in the dark time, they initiate them young people. But we can't see them. Only grandmother can visit them, but not the sister. Because they're still bleeding. This very important, because this is a man job. If any of us woman do wrong thing, we get killed for that. So we dance all night for the young men.

There were rites of passage, too, to mark the changes from girl to woman. Annie remembers the rituals around her own growing up, and is sad young girls miss out now.

These days I think they class themselves like European people, and that been really hard for us mob.

When I was a big woman, now, I was a really woman, my father used to go kill dugong for me. For give to people all over the place, because I'm a woman now, everybody know. Got period, that's the woman now. Finished little girl. And that stop you to walk around. You got to stay there longer. Little bit. You can't eat meat. And the old people used to eat that meat, maybe our father used to kill dugong or turtle, that's for the old people to eat for young girl with first period. They used to make a sacred ground and eat there. We call it marnda marnda. *If you got first period, they got to paint you white everywhere, and say this is a woman now, it's not any more little girl.*

And you can't go in the front of your brother. When your brother get water, you can't drink it. Until you got to go down there yourself and get your own water. Even you get your water, your brother can't take it. Nah. It's the big Law, proper way. That's the sacred Law. But not this day, now.

The ceremonial life that remains intact in the hearts and minds of women like Annie, Thelma and Dinah stretches back to the beginnings of Aboriginal life on the Australian continent.

Spiritual beliefs are inseparable from physical events and all is determined by the sacred Law. There is no European equivalent. The Law was made by spirit ancestors in the creation period, the Dreaming, when they crossed the vast Australian landscape, calling out the names for the hills, valleys, trees, rivers, animals, birds, fish—for everything. They carried the Law with them, and gave this Law for the country to the old people.

The Dreamings were snakes, emu, saltwater crocodile, barramundi, all the animals. They were plants, wind and stars too. The old people sang song cycles that follow the country. They put ceremony on the country. *Nganiyanji barra yarrambawaja jiwini awarala ki Yijandu kujika jilu-manhanji kurdandu narnu-yuwa nyalunga li-rdiyangu li-ngularkaringiu*: they are 'holding the Law intensely' for the new people who come behind. This is the rule of life—to follow the Law and pass it down to every new generation so Dreamings are cared for, country stays strong, season follows season, and people live in balance with each other, their natural environment and the cosmos. Maintaining the Law gave Aboriginal society predictability and security that ordered life brilliantly for tens of thousands of years.

The actions of people in upholding or breaking the Law that the spirit ancestors set down will result in good or bad consequences. If a fish spirit is not properly sung when the fish is speared, the result may be barren hunting in the rivers. If a dugong is harpooned away from a particular clan group's area, or it is not ritually butchered and divided in the right way, the sea can be expected to deliver a punishment—perhaps a boating accident, or a destructive storm. If the wrong people burn land, poor seasons may follow. If a person wears the wrong design at a ceremony a spirit of that place may die, and that land will be weakened, food might be scarce.

People, creatures and nature are entwined in a complex inter-dependent relationship that stirs strong feeling, and draws on both the physical and the mystical. Benevolent and malevolent spirits are an ever-present living reality who interact with the human world, and taking care of Dreaming sites where spirits reside is paramount to maintaining physical health, spiritual balance and emotional stability. A person's identity is tightly bound to his or her human and spirit ancestors, the seasons, the ability to read country and find food, and the knowledge to look after the environment for the next year, the next generation, the next millennium.

People say they can't change the Law of the Dreaming. Musso always said the Law never changes. Because people didn't make it; the Dreamings, the ancestors did. Songs make up maps across country. They are the maps that people carry in their heads, following the paths of creator spirits across the Australian landscape. People leave their bodies, too, Musso told us. He'd travelled across the land and back to his body. Some-times the songs take many days and nights of ceremony to finish singing. Dreaming marks painted on the body for those cer-emonies carry the country, they keep the land and the Dreaming alive. Passing down the songs through ceremony keeps the Dreaming strong. Looking after country protects ceremony. People have to keep the Law going, keep it safe, so ceremony is complete, and land is strong. Country, ceremony and life are inseparable. When people die they are taken back to their country, to send them home to their Dreamings.

People incant the Dreaming in many ways. Painting designs on rock, in the sand or on the body replenishes the stories, keeps them strong. People can also see the physical presence spirit beings left to mark their journeys in the Dreamtime. At

Limiyimyila (Black Craggy Island) you can see a rock in the shape of a canoe that belonged to the spirit dugong hunters who fell down a hole. One had tried to pull the other out with a rope made from the roots of the banyan tree, but he fell in too. There is a red ochre mark on the side of the hole where they fell in.

Along the coast from West Island turtle spirits tried to come ashore to lay their eggs, but it was not their country. The osprey—the sea hawk, *jujuju*—whose Dreaming was at that place, attacked and killed them, and their shells can be seen as rocks on the slope. Jujuju scattered their intestines in another formation of rocks. Stones on the beach at the water's edge are the eggs the turtles began to lay as they scrambled back to the sea. The spirit ancestors' powers are strongest at the places where they created a landform, where a physical representation of them remains, or where they entered the ground or the sea. That power brings alive the land and its creatures. The Dreaming presents a unique way to understand Aboriginal history told the Aboriginal way. Thousands of stories like that of the dugong hunters and the turtle spirits crisscross the Australian continent in a web of songlines that cloak our nation with a net of power and meaning.

The stories of the Dreaming underpin life—where to find food, how to cook, what songs to dance. Baba Thelma remembers with gratitude the knowledge passed down to her by her parents and grandparents; the protocols of sharing, and the value of carrying on the knowledge for people coming behind.

After breakfast we used to go hunting with our parents. So they showed us how to find goanna, how to find blue-tongue. We find goanna on the ground, and blue-tongue too, then we look for bush honey, sugarbag. We know where the sugarbag is. See the bee go in and out, in and out, so we tell that is sugarbag. And then older people used to cut the tree and cut the sugarbag out. So this how we

*learn from the old people. Our people never depend on white people
to teach us. We learn how to speak language.*

*We make a big fire, we cook in the ashes. Cover them, we put
charcoal on top the goanna, so that can cook, make those ashes hot
all the time, so the goanna can cook, or blue-tongue. This what we
used to do. Leg, tail, two side leg. You cut it from the backbone,
open it wide, and then you take that guts out, you don't eat that,
but you can eat liver, and then you share with someone. You cut
it half and share with someone. If someone go with you, you gotta
share that goanna or blue-tongue with them. So this what hunter
always do, and it's very good, and they find their own thing too.
And we share one another the same way. That's good for Aboriginal
people, sharing one another. Because you give, he won't forget you.
He give you back next time, if he get something. So the promise is
the promise. And that true. And we can't eat ourself when someone
just watching us, eating no. We'll feel shame of that. You gotta give
someone that never catch anything.*

*Lily seed. They used to ground up. Also that cycad fruit too. They
used to hit with the stick, wide open, and then they used to get that
inside part, and cut it in slice, dry them out, and put them in sack
bag, throw them to the water for couple of days. So the poison can go
out, so that's what they do. Cook that damper in tea-tree bark, and
bury on the hot ashes. So this how they used to cook some waterlily
seed and that cycad fruit too. It's good.*

Kangaroo, you got to dig the hole, like mungu, *we call it* mungu,
*and you gotta put stone, wood and stone, and then you put the kan-
garoo in, so you can burn that fur off the body, and then you turn it
over, turn it over, then you cut it open, take the guts out, and put the
stone inside, you know, hot rock, so you cook it in the ashes,* mungu.
*Cover that thing with the tea-tree, and put the sand on top of that
tea-tree, so it cook well like stove oven. This what our people do.*

You gonna follow the leader, parents belong to you. Follow, and we used to see how they find things, like sugarbag, goanna. And blue-tongue. And then if that goanna buried in the hole that open, you got to go around and spear the ground, until you get to that end, you break the hole when the goanna is down, and then 'ah, here', right they dig, dig and grab the tail and hit the goanna. Yeah.

Ceremony we used to get good flogging from our people. Like public dance.

'Go for dance. Paint yourself. You not white kid.' They used to talk to us like that. So we used to do that, because we used to get good flogging from our mob, you know, you want to learn your own things. So you can show it to your family later on. That's what they used to say. And we used to go with the older people, paint ourself, so we used to dance with them too. And also dance belong young men—that's different. Clap, different. You just shake leg for public dance. But for tapping your leg, that's when you dance for ceremony, like for young men.

Yanyuwa land offered up a prolific year-round supply of food and medicinal resources if you knew where to find it. Europeans saw an unforgiving and often barren landscape; hot and dusty in the Dry, a torrent of floods in the Wet. Yanyuwa, of course, knew how to harvest and regenerate nature's garden. A-warrangurli was a long, leafy vine with purple grape-like fruit. The seeded fruit, Ma-wnjurrwnjurr, could be eaten straight from the tree, tastes a little like apple, looks like dried plum. Puyukabuyuka and A-kalwakalwa yielded small white berries, and figs from the Alawuma were full of seeds and custard, and tasted like soft cheese. Mayarranja was a soft black fruit like strawberry jam. Ma-lhaba was orange like a mango. The fruit of the cabbage palm, Mujibayi, was eaten from the tree like apples, and yams, A-wuyiku, bush turnips, Wanjiya, bush potato, A-ngardakurr, and pandanus nut, Ma-kurdidi, were prepared and cooked on the ashes.

Ma-kurlulu was the soap tree. Its large, broad leaves and pods lathered up in water to wash with. After boiling it was good to bathe in. Fixed headache, sores and rashes. Ma-marla was boiled up as an ointment for skin complaints.

It was a delicate balance that people trod to blend an increasingly sedentary lifestyle at Malandarri with the longing for bush food and ceremonial life the Law demanded in relation to country. By the 1940s, the connections were fraying to breaking point through three seemingly separate but in fact devastatingly connected factors that snuffed out Yanyuwa control of life on their own lands. The repercussions for culture and the balance of life were catastrophic. The burgeoning cattle industry with its agenda of empire building in the far north and its decimation of hunting environments was taking people further and further from the land they belonged to; the increased distribution of rations and subsequent permanent settlement of older people at Malandarri broke the chain of passing down bush knowledge to young people; and the resulting shift in ceremonial focus from the bush to 'town' weakened ties with Yanyuwa Dreaming places. The scene was set for calamitous, irreparable change.

Europeans—the police, and later the welfare officer—had a vested interest in encouraging people to reside at Malandarri permanently: it provided the ready labour force they needed for surrounding cattle stations. White expansion of the Top End depended on it. With the young people off droving, the lure of rations escalated at Malandarri as elderly people were unable to hunt and gather food for themselves in the bush. And the centre of ceremony shifted geographically. In order of importance, belonging to land is about where you are conceived, where you are born, and where your ceremonies are. With children being born at Malandarri and on cattle stations outside their own country, people stopped going out to traditional Dreaming sites as often as they had not been conceived or born there. Ceremonies were relocated to suit where countrymen were already gathered, particularly the older custodians of ceremony—at or near Malandarri.

The dire consequences of reliance on Europeans that would result in the future were not apparent. The Yanyuwa were by nature resilient, resourceful and open to change. Their trading relationship with the Macassans demonstrated their ability to incorporate new ideas and relationships. So they welcomed new horizons that came with the colonists. The Europeans, though, did not offer a partnership between peers, as the Macassans had. White attitudes of cultural, religious and historical supremacy changed the rules.

A lyrical exception was Roger Jose, possibly the nephew of George Herbert Jose, nineteenth-century Anglican Dean of Adelaide. Roger had arrived in Borroloola by packhorse in 1916, and worked as a labourer mending roads and nearby cattle stations. He brought his Aboriginal wife Maggie back from Darwin in 1927, and achieved folkloric status from his long belted tunics, Maggie's woven pandanus hats that he wore, and the upturned, vine-covered rainwater tank he lived in. A correspondent to officialdom on inequity and custodian of the library, Roger also took Maggie's sister Biddy as his wife, and quoted 'Man's true wealth is the fewness of his needs'.

Most other Europeans in the contact era were vastly less interested than Jose in the wellbeing of locals, and there was widespread blackbirding of Aboriginal people to work the stations—people being sent far from home, with little information about where they were going. Pay was generally just rations and tobacco, sometimes clothes and boots.

Big girl, now, Annie remembers. *Teenage girl. So, I find my husband then. Young girl. I don't know how old. I can't tell you. I can't remember my age. Teenage girl. My husband been take away me from my mother. Long story. Long story. Well, went to Table-land, now. Barkly Tableland we working. Me and my husband. My husband went throughout the country now, mustering, taking all the bullocky, you know, collect all the bullockys around. Then come back to Borroloola again, stay for little while, go again.*

And really, I been with my husband in the bush. You know. Horses. Riding horses. Yeah. My husband used to ride that wild horse, then he used to give me now. I used to work, you know, ride on that wild horse. Someone used to talk 'hey, he might knock you down'. Riding I used to hang on to that horse, yeah. I was a really horsewoman. I learnt myself, ride on my husband horse. He used to buck for me too. I been jump off from the horse. And I grab 'im my son, Johnny, hold that reins. I jumped off all right. I was smart one woman, I was.

All these elements of Borroloola's history, characters and culture were continuing to drive our motivation for the Balarinji business. The studio expanded rapidly in the early 1990s with our work in Japan, and in 1993 we launched our first fashion range in Paris. We'd teamed up on a licence with an Australian company, Ozart, which had connections in Mauritius and in Chamonix, France. Like many people of French background, Ozart director, Mauritian Jano Couacaud, was fascinated by Indigenous art and culture, and the landscapes which inspired it. He also had a sublime eye for the Balarinji photographic catalogues he shot with Indigenous and European models in the Red Centre and on the Great Barrier Reef. These award-winning publications depicted an Australian fashion story never before seen on the world stage.

Our jeans, leggings, shirts, dresses and T-shirts found buyers in French holiday destinations as far afield as the Caribbean, the Pacific and the Mediterranean coast. Borroloola family members Roy Hammer, Barry John and Tom Simon came with us to France. They played the didgeridoo at trade fairs and in Parisian bars. And they enjoyed a glass of Bordeaux red with their fillet steak in trendy brasseries. We released collections with Ozart again in Paris the following year, and a third time in 1996 at the famous Prêt-à-Porter fashion show.

With Balarinji collections making waves in both Japan and Europe, we began to think about how to accelerate our goals to tell our design story in Australia. Our base in Adelaide was distant from our eastern seaboard markets in Melbourne and Sydney. Although we were collecting awards and recognition in our small home state, it was not translating to a national profile, and our aim of signaturing Australia.

Earlier in 1993, before we'd launched our first collection in Paris, I'd woken at 2 am with an idea. I'd shaken John awake, and said we should paint a Qantas jumbo jet with our designs. John had been lukewarm about both the time of the night and the implausibility of the idea. He told me Qantas, still government-owned at the time, simply wouldn't do it. Go back to sleep, he said.

But it made perfect sense. Qantas was the pinnacle of Australian brands. If Qantas took us to heart, so might the nation. We made a visual presentation by painting art on a clear acetate overlay for a large poster of a Qantas 747. We decided the palette should be red, and the story should be kangaroo, John's totem. We didn't simply want to use the fuselage as an advertising billboard, and we knew it wouldn't interest the airline. We wanted to fly an unprecedented statement about being Australian that also captured the essence of Qantas, and we needed an idea that would be irresistible to them.

The late Mick Young, former Labor Senator, was on the board of Qantas, and knew John from the Aboriginal rights fight of the 1960s. Mick was happy to be our conduit to Qantas management. We were able to send in the poster we'd created, and a model we'd handpainted. The response, though, was minimal, and as John had predicted the idea sat gathering dust in a Qantas office somewhere in Mascot near Sydney Airport. Over the next few months, we'd occasionally rack our brains about how to move it along, but the day-to-day of the business didn't leave much time for speculating on 'dead leads'.

We did get one chance, though, to try another angle. John was travelling often for clients and his work on government boards by that time, and Qantas invited us to a frequent-flyer weekend at Adelaide's Hyatt Hotel in May 1994. They wanted feedback from passengers at the coalface. Our opportunity came on the final morning. We took the lift down to the ground floor with CEO James Strong and his wife Jeanne-Claude. While John delayed them at the bottom, I raced back to our room to fetch a copy of the poster we had created. I showed it to James in the foyer. He smiled in surprise but, though polite, didn't seem to engage.

Then, out of the blue, we got a call from Garry Saunders, the marketing director on whose desk the model had been sitting for more than a year.

'Remember the model you did with Aboriginal design on it?'

he said. 'Well, we think we might want to do it. I'd like to come to Adelaide to talk with you.'

I put my hand over the mouthpiece, screamed, regained my composure, and told him calmly that we'd be happy to meet. I'd had spinal surgery for a ruptured disc the week before, and this was better than the painkillers.

Qantas needed to race Ansett to the opening of the new Kansai airport in Osaka. It was to be Ansett's first international flight, and Qantas wanted to protect its share of the lucrative Japanese market. Garry asked if we thought our aircraft would attract the press; they wanted to upstage Ansett's inaugural flight. We assured them the Japanese would vote with their cameras, and suggested we take a group of elders and dancers from Borroloola on the flight.

A few weeks later, the paint job was in full swing. Our model was computerised and magnified a hundred times to produce two kilometres of tracing paper. The motifs were serrated to form a stencil, and the tracing paper was wrapped around the fuselage of the newest state-of-the-art 747-400 airliner in the Qantas fleet. For thirteen days, a crew of engineers, painters and technicians worked secretly around the clock in Sydney Airport's Hangar 245 to roller, brush and spray six hundred litres of brilliantly coloured expandable paint onto the aircraft. The green of the Wet season, blue-purple of mountain ridges at dusk, yellow ochre of sand-stone country, charcoal of campfires and white ochre of body paint shimmered on the red base of the design. Kangaroos leapt across songlines and campsites that wrapped around the aircraft's belly in the way we wanted their meaning to wrap around the nation.

Wunala (Kangaroo) Dreaming was rolled out onto the tarmac to face the country's media on 4 September 1994.

The power of it left a lot of jaws on the ground. Robert Tickner, Minister for Aboriginal Affairs, called it a beacon for reconciliation. It struck an immediate chord with Australians of all ages and backgrounds, and by the time we were winging our way to Osaka on the inaugural flight we'd already scored nationwide press. When it touched down in Kansai that evening, our marketing mission was more than delivered. Qantas had requested a bay next to Ansett, and had pulled out all stops to arrive half an hour earlier than its competitor. As passengers disembarked from Ansett, they were rushing to the air-bridge windows to photograph Qantas. The *Yomiuri Shimbun* newspaper, circulation 10 million, published us in colour, generating $5 million in publicity in just one afternoon. Wunala went on to become the most photographed aircraft in the world, featuring in newspapers, magazines, websites and television broadcasts everywhere.

John always described seeing the film of the aircraft later, coming into Kansai, as among his favourite Wunala moments. As she emerged from the grey Osaka sky her colours came gradually into vivid focus, like a butterfly emerging from its cocoon. When she touched down, our Borroloola crew—Roy, Tom and Barry— were first off the plane. In full body paint and adorned with feathers and ceremonial belts, they danced a corroboree in the terminal for the stunned world media gathered for the opening. It was almost beyond belief that the Australia that had taken John away from his family and forbidden him to speak in language or hunt or make spears was now heralding his culture on the world stage.

John said he melted inside when he first saw the plane that day.

It's a feeling you don't get very often—it makes you feel humble, elated, secure. It makes you feel all those things. It's happiness, I suppose.

Letters, phone calls and personal comments from all over Australia and the world continue to tell us of the depth of positive feeling that Wunala stirs. Life offers up euphoric moments from time to time. The emotion of creating Wunala Dreaming was one.

7

Truth

ihaanjima
Beauty is when I am straight with my integrity.

Truth is a tranquil pool in my soul. When I keep my integrity, that's when I know the inner beauty of my spirit.

Day 7, Thursday 1 June 2006

*Y*uwani Annie wakes as usual at sunrise. I listen to her call.

'Today is the last day. Good morning.' She sings in language, sitting up on her mattress, blankets wrapped around herself against the cold dawn. But there is no wind. The eastern horizon is a strip of rich orange. Tree trunks are silhouetted. The morning star has not yet faded.

The morning routine is soothing. I sit up in my swag. The women who are already sitting up call to me. It is a language test.

'Good morning, Baba,' I call. 'Good morning, Manjigarra, good morning, Yuwani, good morning, Kathakatha.'

Just one error. Marrawarra—my cousin—Edna Pluto corrects me gently when I greet her as sister-in-law. A smile— 'That's all right'—to my apology. Edna is the last living grandmother, Kukurdi, for John.

Whatever ideas I had about researching this book have become redundant. I realise that the wisdom I want to articulate will not be found in the answers to my questions. It is wrapped in the rituals I am seeing this week, in the love that is being sent across the camp in morning greetings, in the communion of touch when rubbing skin with ochres and oils. It is deep within the language, where translation reveals both the common humanity and the philosophical divide between the black and white faces of Australia.

There is jubilation this morning from Kathakatha Isa, my dance teacher. A tight hug and a kiss on my cheek as we link arms and walk together towards the start of the morning rituals. 'Good dancer,' she lies encouragingly. I feel an unexpected surge of love for her. Her love for me is contagious.

I check my eyes out in the side mirror of the car. They look as puffy and congested from the desert dust as they feel. I slather sunscreen on my face and neck.

By mid-morning there is some urgency about ceremony that remains to be finished before the camp is dismantled. Desert women are already on the dancing ground. Yuwani Annie wants to go out and sit. But she is tired. She lies down on her mattress. 'I'm going to sleep.' It has been six days since we left Borroloola, almost two of those days on the road. Up early, long hours. Preparation, waiting, practising, dancing, stories. The older women are stiff now when they sit down and get up. But their happiness at being together, to carry out the Business, observe the Rules, overrides the exhaustion.

Word is out that today's food bags will have kangaroo tail. Popular choice. It is 10.30 am. The camp is quietly settled, patiently waiting again. A card game starts up. It has complicated arithmetic. The players are sharp. I think about the things I have brought—what didn't I need? My bag of clothes could mostly go. A shirt and a spare I need, my bush hat to stop my face frying up, and I like my toothbrush with the sweet freshness of mint. The rest is clutter. I feel relaxed and alive without it.

It is nearly midday, and there is no preparation in the Borroloola camp yet. Maybe we won't dance until tonight, they are saying. Dark would be good. I will grill out there under the desert sun. And I'm conscious that my body will be neon white in a sea of black skin made for this desert country.

Yuwani Annie sleeps peacefully in the shade on her mattress next to me. The cough mixture seems to be working. Baba Rosie is resting on the tarp on the other side. I am using my rolled-up swag as a seat—a rest for my aching bones and joints.

It is the last day. Time to bring out my last shirt. It is white, but it will be red from the dust in a few minutes. My nails are putrid—red sand, red ochre and black charcoal. My palms are clean from frequent washing that fails to lift the dirt from the backs of my hands and my nails.

The kangaroo tails arrive in long individual plastic bags. Like baguettes—with fur. They are seared in the flames, then wrapped in foil. The coals of the fire are raked aside, foiled tails laid on the clearing, the coals heaped back over, and cooked for half an hour. They are distributed and set aside with relish for tomorrow's drive home. We sample a few delicious chunks, hot from the fire. We eat the tender meat and discard the charred skin.

I am talking to Thelma about some words in Yanyuwa when the call goes out to get ready for ceremony. It is now, not tonight. Red ochre is mixed in oil and rubbed into our skin. Body paint is carefully applied on top, cool and refreshing. Headbands are tied, and we wait. I wait with the Nangala women, my skin group. There is a buzz of excitement.

We are called, and the Borroloola ceremony dancing and songs begin. The other skin group first. Annie's familiar voice rings out across the gathering of a hundred women seated on the ground, watching. Baba Rosie sings too. Clap sticks carry the beat. The dancers' movements are subtle, rhythmic. The melody is tuneful, haunting.

Now it's the Nangala skin's turn. Kathakatha Linda positions me next to her in the dancing line. 'Watch me, Narna,' she whispers as we move out towards the ceremony ground. It feels more connected than last night's practice. Somehow they take me with them, and I feel the beat in my body. They have generously wrapped me among them—not tagged me on the end as the new one. Or the white one. We move through the rituals. Secret. Sacred. Symbols, objects. 'Make you strong,' I can hear Annie's voice saying in my head as I move. The privilege of inclusion is humbling.

Later, Kathakatha Isa, my dance teacher, gives me a warm hug. 'Borroloola winner, Narna.' I know my lack of accomplishment would have been obvious. But many of the women convey their enthusiastic approval: I have been through 'the Business' for the first time. They are genuinely happy for me. Their gift to me is belonging.

It is the last night tonight. There are mixed emotions in the camp.

'We're going home,' Annie says.

I ask them if it feels good to be going home.

'Yeah,' they say with emphasis. 'But good here too. Too much humbug at home. Too many drunks.'

I ask Annie how they can stop the grog.

'I dunno. Them all drinkin'.' Then she laughs. 'I used to drink big mob rum. Big fighter, me. Now I only chew tobacca. Makes me cough, but I like it.' She mentions one of the young men who is drinking too much, shaking her head at the problem. Then her face creases into a smile, and she says, 'But I *love* that boy!'

I try to write in snatches of moments out here in the desert. I don't want to embellish or dilute the experience. It is perfect the way it is. I am afraid I won't remember the details, the nuances.

I go to bed early. It's a long journey tomorrow, and there is no-one to share the driving. There is singing most of the night. I drift in and out of sleep. The singing is a lullaby in this sandy cocoon of red dirt and ebony sky. I wake suddenly in the early hours of the morning. Annie has fallen. She has tried to get up from her mattress, and has stumbled. I grab my torch and call to her.

'I'm all right,' she says. 'My foot, that's all.' She has been suffering painful blisters from tight second-hand shoes. I haven't heard a word of complaint from her all week, nor from any of the other frail older women.

CHANGES THAT THE CATTLE industry had wrought in the Gulf led to the long-term chasm that would deny people like Annie both their roots from the past and a stake in the flourishing future that Australia was forging. By the mid-twentieth century, 'too many bullocky' were polluting waterholes, trampling nutritious seeds and berries, and destroying the habitats of freshwater turtle and other small game. Overgrazing was causing fresh water to dry up earlier in the winter season, and the landforms known so intimately to the Yanyuwa were changing from the chronic erosion of loose alluvial soils from cattle eating the country bare. People were being forced to stay longer in town to find something to eat. The tug of ceremonial ties to land, and the pull of life in town with its ready supply of flour, tea and tobacco, made for a seesaw of loaded choices.

John was born in the bush near Malandarri around 1938, in the middle of this time of upheaval and transition. Only a handful of Europeans found their way to the Gulf in those years, including John's Irish father, John Moriarty, and cousins who ran the Borroloola Pub, the O'Sheas. The European population of Borroloola numbered no more than eight or ten between 1900 and 1960, and the Aboriginal population in and near town fluctuated from a handful to a couple of hundred. The Borroloola police letter book documents the reluctance of officers to be posted there, including the graphic story of one policeman who suicided after his pleas to be moved were ignored. To all but the Yanyuwa, Gudanji, Marra and Garrawa, it was unnerving, isolated country. The road to Borroloola led to nowhere else and the mail service came in just once a month, by truck in the Dry and on horseback in the Wet. Incoming telegrams could be heard over the wire, but could only be sent in morse.

The arrival of John Moriarty from Ireland on this scene was as improbable as it was romantic. It was difficult for John to put the pieces together, as he had no recollection of his father and Kathleen hardly spoke of him. Yet he had a hunger to find him. It wasn't until January 1981, more than twenty years after he reconnected with his mother and on his second trip to Ireland, that John found his father's family in County Kerry, on the ruggedly beautiful south-west coast. Scouring telephone books for Moriartys in Kerry led him to John Moriarty, the undertaker at Castle Gregory.

John the undertaker was unrelated, but he made some calls and his son Sean took John to see ninety-two-year-old Paddy O'Shea, who lived nearby. They thought there might be a connection with the O'Sheas who'd turned up in Borroloola. Paddy fired a few questions and sized John up on the porch for some time before asking him in from the bitter cold. Satisfied with what he'd heard,

Paddy brought a brown paper package out from the cupboard. Inside was a cane fishing rod and a reel.

'Your father and I went fishing for three days just before he sailed for Australia,' he said. 'This rod is yours. Your father left it here fifty-two years ago.'

Back at his house, over a hearty lamb dinner with a great deal of potato and a very large whisky, John Moriarty the undertaker suggested John call John Moriarty of Racecourse Road in Tralee, twenty-eight miles away. If Paddy O'Shea was right, the man from Tralee would be John's first cousin, the son of John's father's brother, Daniel. John remembers an odd conversation by phone that went something like: 'Is that John Moriarty? This is John Moriarty from Australia. I am looking for my father John Moriarty. John Moriarty here in Castle Gregory suggested I ring you.' The John Moriarty on the other end of the phone confirmed that his uncle, John Moriarty, had indeed gone to Australia, and at his house later that day John pored over some photos. And there it was—a picture of the Borroloola pub with John's mother standing on the verandah. John Moriarty of Racecourse Road pointed out a lean, athletic-looking man in the foreground. 'That's my uncle,' he said, and then John was sure.

The two Johns went to a tiny cottage in nearby windswept Blennerville, to meet their uncle Eugene Moriarty, the brother of both their fathers. He told John that his father had lived with him, his brother Joe and their parents in the thatch-roofed family home by the Blennerville wharf before he left Ireland. It was where the ships had set sail for America in the desperate years of the potato famine, and where John's father had boarded his ship to Australia in 1928 after a failed love affair had broken his heart.

Eugene told John his father had written to his mother in Blennerville every week from Australia, and showed him the room where the letters and postcards were piled up in a heap on the floor, reaching halfway up the wall. John was reticent about asking to look at them more closely, and just three months after his visit Eugene passed away, the letters and cards presumably discarded when the house was cleared. Whether those letters told his grandmother of his existence and what they said about his father's Australian odyssey John will never know, but it was enough to make the connection.

John often smiles about what his Irish relatives might have thought about him rolling up on the doorstep, their black cousin and nephew from Australia. He was, though, profoundly grateful and relieved to find them, and had the deepest sleep of his life at John Moriarty and his wife Morna's house in Race-course Road the night he tracked his father down.

The relationship between John and Kathleen that bore baby John was illegal. Which I guess made John, with incriminating skin that was paler than his mother's, illegal too. It is unlikely his father was still in the Gulf when the welfare and the church took John away. There is scant information about him, apart from a death certificate from the Queensland Registry of Births, Deaths and Marriages establishing he died of lung cancer in Brisbane in 1961. John had a lot of press in Brisbane in 1961, playing a soccer match for South Australia against Queensland. Sometimes John wonders—with a touch of longing, I think—if his father ever saw his photo or noticed his name.

The memory of police coming around looking for half-caste children is fresh in the minds of the older generation at Borroloola. John's tribal sister, Peggy, was just a baby when her mother Emmalina rolled her up in a swag, begging her not to cry until the policeman had gone away. They missed Peggy that time, but got her not long after. She grew up in Victoria and married in South Australia, returning to Borroloola only after she'd had children of her own and her white husband Trevor encouraged her to trace her links back to her family. Mothers of children taken away cut themselves, like women do for 'sorry business', for funerals. Their grief knew no end, as many never saw their children again.

It was during the Second World War, in 1942, that John was loaded onto the back of the army truck at just four years of age and transported south. Although he'd meet his mother briefly in Alice Springs eleven years later, and his uncle Musso in Darwin in the 1960s, it would be more than thirty years before he returned to his Borroloola family, in the early 1970s.

For the first eight years of his exile, John lived in Mulgoa at the foot of Sydney's Blue Mountains, an inmate of a mission home run by the Anglican Church. It was a bizarre place to bring small Aboriginal children with no English, and no knowledge of life beyond their tropical bush camps. The regime was hunger, religion and discipline. John has taken us there to stroll around. He's pointed out the little Mulgoa School where he walked barefoot in the frost, and told us about discovering white kids had bread that wasn't hard and dry like the crusts he scavenged from the bins. The war was impacting the church's finances, and they had little money to feed and clothe the Aboriginal children being delivered from the north. Shoes with gaping holes in the soles and no underwear made the mountain winters even colder.

The agenda was abandonment of culture and acceptance of Jesus Christ. John feels Aboriginal people in any case live a heightened spiritual life, and later, like many others, he failed to see the conflict between Christianity and his own ceremonial inheritance. The Church, though, had no such tolerance, and strictly forbade speaking in language or continuing Aboriginal ways.

It would have been like stopping breathing, so the children spoke names from home softly and roamed the countryside making little spears, catching small game or fish, gathering berries and roots of grasses from the bush, throwing a rock to stun a rabbit or a bird they could cook on the coals when they were starving.

As we sat around a fire in Mount Wilson one trip up there, John heating and honing a spear he'd cut down, he remembered the things that continued away from the missionaries' eyes. With a scar on his forehead to show for it, John described their spear-throwing games. The bigger boys had to face an oncoming blunt-ended spear, and deflect it with a bundle of spears they were holding. Seven- or eight-year-old John had been proud his scar was not from battle, where he wanted to excel like a man, like a warrior. He was hit by a stray spear as he walked back to stand in the throwing line.

A number of children had been brought down with John from Borroloola and Roper River, as well as some slightly older girls who became cooks and housekeepers. Those girls took on a mothering role, gave them all hope, kept talking about the families at home. They never let the younger ones forget who they were. They sang beautifully in church, and their love, and the love he could find elsewhere around him, kept John going. Like the chickens he tended. They'd let him pick them up, stroke them and cuddle them. Sometimes they'd lay eggs in his hands.

A few smaller boys, including John, slept in the stone cellar as there was no room for them in the house, a convict-built rectory next to St Thomas's. John remembers it as cold, dank and terrifying. The boys were told that convicts had been chained up in there and tortured. The sandstone block that seeped dripping water onto the prisoner tied underneath was still there. One night, in the pitch-black, John heard hobnailed boots pacing the floor in the furthest, darkest part of the cellar where his relation Boofa was sleeping. Petrified, he stayed awake, his head lifted off the pillow, not moving, hardly breathing, for what felt like hours, ashamed he was too frightened to get out of bed. He was a bit surprised but hugely relieved to find Boofa safe and sound in the morning.

When he was nine or ten, John was moved further up the mountains with two of the other younger boys to leafy Mount Wilson. John remembers with gratitude those few months in the home of Reverend Harry Dormer and his wife. In Mrs Dormer's ample kitchen he discovered the indescribable delights of roast dinners, butter, blackberry pie and cream, loganberries and scones. The natural world of that part of the mountains entranced him too, with its black snakes, all sorts of birds and tiny sparks of light that were fireflies in the night. Snow fights and snowmen were another magnificent part of his stay in Mount Wilson. But it was not to last, and he was soon back in the dormitory in Mulgoa. He felt the same sadness as when he'd been taken away from the Gulf. He was still only ten years old and he knew Mrs Dormer had loved him. And he'd loved her. John never forgot Mrs Dormer— he went to her funeral in Sydney in 2008.

Things suddenly changed again not long after the younger boys returned from Mount Wilson. The church in Mulgoa ran out of money, and in January 1949 the children were loaded onto the train out of Sydney. The girls were bound for a home in Alice Springs. The boys were sent to St Francis House in Semaphore, Adelaide, which had just been established by an Anglican priest, Father Percy McDonald Smith. John was devastated to leave the mountains just as he had begun to come to terms with his new life. He remembers leaning out of the carriage at Sydney's Central Station, trying in vain not to let the tears come, farewelling his best friend Brian Walker, a local boy, and his brother Ken, who'd travelled to the city to see the train go. He missed Brian, and he missed the young women singing in church. Looking back, he thinks missing the lovely voices of those women so badly was the pent-up longing he had for his mother and his grandmother. And the wondering if he would ever see them again.

In Adelaide John was given his first set of underwear, and his first dressing-gown. He was also given plenty of lashings with a rubber hose when the morning bell rang to herd the boys down the stairs to breakfast. He washed regularly in hot water for the first time, and his stomach was empty less often. There was already a contingent from Alice Springs at St Francis House, boys whose parents had sent them there to school, and the pecking-order fights began. John copped a few bloody noses, but won some of those fights too. He was happy to have some bigger boys like Wally McArthur stick up for him. Jobs in the kitchen meant better pickings from the food on offer, and John was always a willing volunteer.

Father Smith's mother-in-law, Mrs Almond, lived at St Francis House too. She was quite incapacitated, John recalls, and over-weight. The boys were at times required to carry her between rooms, or up and down stairs. One day they dropped her. Doubled up with laughter, but scared of the repercussions, they fled. She tried to whack them from the floor with her walking stick, but they were too quick for her. John always said he had no complaints about Father Smith. That he treated him well. Father Taylor, though, who succeeded him, was cruel with the hose, and Father Sherwin, after Taylor, got the boys' clothes from the army disposal store and dressed them all in khaki like little soldiers, and had them stand to attention for 'parade'. John says he was a nut.

The boys whose parents had sent them to St Francis House

had a little money, and went on holidays and had bikes—unlike the Mulgoa boys, who had no money at all, ran the three miles to and from school, and were completely reliant on welfare. They'd watch the others go off at Christmas, and spend the weeks of school holidays mucking around on Semaphore beach, spearing some fish in the shallows, running through the sandhills. They had nothing, and there were small kindnesses that John never forgot. Like his Year 7 teacher, Mr Nelson, who quietly paid for him to go on an excursion when he'd been too embarrassed to admit he didn't have four shillings for the fare. And Mr Nelson must have suspected he didn't have sandwiches from home either, because he took him to his parents' place in Mallala for lunch.

John excelled at Aussie Rules, rubgy, cricket and soccer, and at school. His love of Henry Lawson, Banjo Paterson and Shake-speare made no difference, though, as after primary school he was shunted into a technical school. There was no contemplation of higher education or university for Aboriginal students. It was something John would come to much later in his life.

At the other end of the country, the destiny of John's family was playing out without him. The entire world of the Yanyuwa was con-tinuing to change beyond recognition. Both the cattle industry and the war had resulted in the relocation of people across hundreds of square kilometres of country. A systematic clearing of Yanyuwa land on the coast and upriver for security resulted in people being scattered far from their lands and connections. People often had no idea where other family members were. Those remaining in the region worked and lived as best they could between stations, the bush and Borroloola.

Annie remembers coming in and out of Borroloola, settling there, and having her children in the late 1940s. It paralleled the life of John's mother and that of most young married people in the area.

At the police station I used to work ironing, and doing other thing, washing along machine, washing all the clothes. And now I know my job. Collect everythings together, wash everything for that whitefella, for that policeman. He brought us down now here, Borroloola. We used to work at Robinson (River Station) too. Washing dishes and all that. I used to housekeeper—that's what I was. Housekeeper. Every station I been, yeah, I know all my jobs. Hard labour too. Doing everythings for them. Set the table, the right way, we used to do. Right way. White man's way. Now finish now, we come back here now. We stay here now along Borroloola.

Too many children. Don't tell me. First one mine, Johnny Isaac. Then from there, Irene. Irene married along whitefella. Anne. Eunice. And Michael. One was drowned here. His name was Darcy. He was a big boy, and had sickness too. Floodwater time. Floodwater took him. Mmm. I got Michael, David Isaac. Who else? Louise. That's all. Three woman and three men too. Bush way. All born bush way. I had in the bush. Not in Darwin in the hospital. (Holiday time) used to walk around in the islands, Bing Bong way, everywhere. When we come back now on welfare time, we never used to walk around now. Welfare used to stop us. Because welfare been send us to station. True.

In the heyday of station employment right up until the 1950s, the police and welfare would organise trucks at the beginning of each Dry season to take workers from Malandarri to the stations. Almost everyone loaded up and headed to the cattle. Only the very old, the sick and pregnant women who'd previously had difficult births were left behind.

Despite its hardships, injustices and violence, the Yanyuwa see 'cattle times' as another experience in their lives, and look back on it as a comparatively happy period. Particularly the men, as the work meant being out bush, using their bush skills, often with some independence. Tracking and finding water were second nature to them in those landscapes. Without their skills, their European masters and their herds would have perished. 'Cattle times' heritage is evident still, in the slick performances of the cowboy-hatted riders at Borroloola's rodeo every August.

Lighting fires with sticks and making bark bridles when leather was not available kept the old stock camps operational. Aboriginal stockmen also found enough in common with their European and Chinese co-workers to enjoy a more egalitarian attitude than they'd experienced with police and other white authorities they were coming into contact with.

Women have mixed memories, as few joined their husbands at the stock camps. Some who did recall riding like the fury with a baby strapped to their chest, and tying their children safely up in a tree while they threw wild bulls. Most women were confined to the stations, raising children as well as cleaning and cooking for their European bosses. With their husbands often away for long periods droving, they were frequently subjected to sexual exploitation by white men.

Thelma worked hard and enjoyed this time with her husband.

On McArthur River Station, I used to do cleaning, sometime cooking for the stockmen. Helping one of the lady there working. I had my three childrens up there. Debra, and my other son pass away. And Ronald. So they all from that place, and I think Ian born in Borroloola. We came back here, because we been there too long.

My husband been stockman. Got up early on the station, before sunrise, and cook for everybody. We used to ring the bell for them, have breakfast, and after that they used to saddle their horse and go.

So that's been a hard life too. And they used to go for muster, long way, come back in the evening. They used to carry their dinner too. Yeah.

Well we used to do laundry for manager and his wife. Wash their clothes, sheet, hang them. And we used to go back home then. Nice place. We used to have bed, blanket-swag. Good food. Sometime they used to kill for us when they used to go out. Leave some meat for us. And they used to go away, mustering. Sometimes I was riding all day too. Till in the evening. You gotta ride a horse all the time. And get there in the afternoon. Stop, cook some food.

For the men, there was much to learn from the spiritual activities that continued at the stock camps. While most were far away from their own lands, evenings were often spent around the campfire listening to the Dreaming stories from those old men whose land they were travelling through. Managers would generally not intrude if people took a couple of days off for a ceremony in particular places. Men also felt while droving they were carrying out their expected roles of messengers across landscape. And their traditional prestige as hunters and providers of meat was retained thanks to the ready supply of cattle to be killed.

In 1948 the police station in Borroloola closed and a permanent welfare officer was appointed. Welfare was a powerful force in town, as the welfare officer held the key to the ration store. By now, not only the elderly were receiving rations, but the general community as well. And the commodities had extended to flour, tea, sugar, salt beef, potatoes, rice, rolled oats, soap and blankets. Withholding of rations was used to control and punish—for example, if children were dirty or people challenged the authority of the welfare officer.

It was intentionally paternalistic, and the clearly stated government policy was assimilation of Aboriginal people into white ways.

Life was highly regulated under the regime of the welfare. A siren or bell before sun-up marked the start of the working day, and people paddled across the river from Malandarri to the 'white side' at Borroloola, to begin work in the welfare officer's household: men tending gardens and women cooking and cleaning. The welfare officer's wife conducted sewing and cooking classes, and mothers brought their babies across for formula feeds. Ceremonial activities were discouraged by most welfare officers; Aboriginal customs were seen as an impediment to the transition from black society to white, particularly as they restricted time available for employment. In the cattle season, welfare had the power to send people away without question to work on any station, anywhere, that needed labour, regardless of the conditions and treatment Aboriginal people would find there. Annie was at the centre of a brutal event that marked a turning point in the cruelty and autocracy meted out by some station managers.

We used to work at Eva Downs. We had a problem there, then. Get out of there. I don't know what his name now. I forget 'im, that name. That whitefella you know. Jealousing people. Cheeky people they used to be at Eva Downs Station. Manager. Well, he used to belt all the boy, my husband and another one. We went to court, at Tennant Creek. Policeman came around and pick us up. Welfare too. Went to Darwin. Big place. Now we put that man away in jail. He was too cheeky. He went to jail now.

'Cheeky' translates not as playful, but as 'poisonous' or 'bad'. This incident Annie describes occurred not at the turn of the century in some sort of colonial conflict, but in 1956. It was the year I was born into a quiet, secure family. It was the year Australia paraded its community before the world at the Melbourne Olympic Games. And it was the year the courage of these Yanyuwa and Garrawa people, including Annie, who were brutally whipped at Eva Downs Station, marked the turning point of race relations in the Northern Territory. They feared they would be shot and put in a hole that had been dug after the beatings, and people told they'd gone bush. So they walked a hundred kilometres across country to escape. A conviction was recorded, and Europeans had to accept that they could not chain and hobble Aboriginal people like animals any longer, and Aboriginal people realised they did not have to take it.

Missionaries arrived relatively late in Borroloola, in the 1950s, but quickly set about prohibiting and further weakening traditional practices. There was some competition with the welfare, whom the missionaries thought had become too familiar with the locals, some of them even adopting 'native ways' or turning a blind eye to heathen practices.

In their disdain of arranged marriages, particularly when polygamous or between old men and young girls, the missionaries gave their blessing to wrong-way relationships, oblivious to the breakdown in elders' authority that this precipitated. Young people found an ally in the church to flout the rigorous structures of traditional life that had served their society well for generations. Thelma was one of them.

Got married my husband in Borroloola. Wrong skin. He's been a Bangarrinji man, and me Nangala, so when he was ready to go back to the station, he came back and got me over here, and we just went on to McArthur River. Everybody, not only me, did that.

In order to discourage black and white co-habitation, and the resulting evidence of half-caste kids, young men heading to the stations were often encouraged to 'grab a girl' as a wife to take along with him.

Missionaries believed they'd stopped people holding ceremonies. Annie said they told her, *Don't dance. Don't sing him.*

She'd reply, 'Well, we're not white people.' That's the way I talk. 'We can sing our own corroboree because we black . . . we can't understand you, too.'

Annie said that ceremonies continued *without the missionary knowing . . . hide it . . . at Malandarri.* She saw contradictions in the teachings of the church. Abraham was circumcised, so why did they try to stop the practice among the Yanyuwa? And why did missionaries tell them to have only one wife, when there were plenty of men in the Bible with many?

Annie also ignored the church's calls for abstinence from alcohol.

When I used to drink, I used to mordu, *crazy. True. Anything I used to drink. Hundred proof rum. Really strong rum. We never used to drink this beer. The first time now. Strong drink we used to have. Fight everything, everywhere. Fight all the whitefella. I used to be good fighter. Frighten all the womens around. I fight men, too, you know. With a nulla nulla. Yeah. I mad proper, when I was young. True.*

I used to go argument whitefellas at the pub. I used to argue with welfare. Used to argument policeman. Policeman took me out there, out bush, because I used to say I could fight anybody around. All right, you good fighter. Anyhow, I'll take you. He took me out to the graveyard, he dropped me out there. I came back walking, walking, from out there. One old whitefella used to live there, Gibson, his name, and he give me drink of tea, when I been walkin' home. This is my story. Really.

Thelma corroborates the story.

This mob used to drink. They used to leave the children, you know, crying behind, nobody there to feed them. We used to see them. They look terrible. They can't understand where they are, what they doing. She—Annie—been the worst one. Then police-man took her down to cemetery. Leave her there. She come back. Ha . . . got lot of goanna and blue-tongue on the way home.

Thelma recalls her childhood, the coercion to stay in town for rations and the growing presence of the welfare and missionaries.

I was in McArthur River Station. I born there, but I grew up Borroloola. My mother brought me back here. Because my mother and my stepmother, they got married one husband, my dad. Yeah. Every old people here, they used to marry two wife or three wife. So this what happened.

I remember that we used to just swim across this river, like after the school. They used to bring us by canoe across the river, this side, and we used to walk from the jetty up to school. We went to mission school. Where the church is now. That's where we used to go to school. The missionary from Sydney came, Mr Pattemore. And his wife. They used to teach us here, learn how to read and write. So this been a good days, without no grog.

They never let people go away from here. Too far, because you got to wait here for ration. Every Friday we used to get ration. Our parents, then young people like us mob. We did a job around Borroloola. Like cleaning up, some used to work outside kitchen, some they were house girl, you know. We used to work at the welfare. They used to teach us how to cook, how to serve, how to set the table.

I used to look after goat, at old police station. Two women used to have a holiday, Saturday and Sunday. The children used to go herd the goat, sometime ride the goat. One of those welfare flog us, me and the other girl, maybe Jemima. From riding the goat and from drinking the milk. This what we used to do. Every Saturday, Sunday.

Jemima remembers the Pattemore missionaries too.

I been come into Borroloola. I went to school. When Mr and Mrs Pattemore were here. They had two girl, Joy and Dorothy. And boy, David. Three kids been born here. That Mrs Pattemore never go to Darwin Hospital. She have her sister-in-law fly from Sydney, be a nurse for her. One of them old ladies help too.

162

I had two kids in the bush, and four at the hospital. Bush better. Because that's our life. We never know hospital.

This balance of sorts was continuing to operate, with families trying to keep up some aspects of tradition on bush lands, but the threads were continuing to unravel. The ways of the welfare and the church were having their intended effect.

8

Grief

jarna-rarrinji ngililiji
Worth is when I can cry for people.

Crying matters. When I cry with tears for other people
I know the goodness inside me.

*t*he plan to set out soon after dawn is thwarted by some unfinished business on the ceremony ground. It takes an hour or more in the cold morning air. Then the new ones—the ones who have gone through the Business for the first time, including me—are rubbed with red ochre. It is for protection. So we don't get sick from the strong ceremony. The ceremony ground is cleared. The vehicles are stamped all over with red ochre hand prints, to protect everyone leaving this place. We each put on a red headband made of strands of wool—a modern replacement for the woven human hair of the past. I can tell these things because it will be public for all to see in just a few hours.

The convoy of twenty-five four-wheel drives and a bus winds it way slowly out of the ceremony ground. I watch for any protruding sticks in the undergrowth that might burst my tyres again. We make it out onto the dirt road, and put enough distance between each other to avoid the thick clouds of red dust being thrown up by the tyres in front. We move slowly. Quiet singing fills our car.

The four of us are gnawing on pieces of kangaroo tail. We are hungry, and the flesh is succulent, flavoursome. Thelma peels back the singed fur so I can eat it easily while driving.

First stop is Kalkaringi sports oval. Maybe a hundred and fifty people sit on the ground, waiting for us. Their backs are to us, women on one side, men on the other. We drive in and park in a semicircle behind them. There are at least a hundred and fifty women still in the convoy, observing the Law to be received back into the community after ceremony. We walk together behind the lines of seated people, singing, ochre and paint still on our bodies. We brush the heads and shoulders of the seated people with leafy branches. The men walk away, and the women and children move in a procession towards us. We shake hands firmly with each of them in turn. Warmth comes back to each of us in their eyes and smiles. Once again, as has happened so many times this week, I feel very emotional. I feel humbled by the power of human connection when material things are stripped away. Almost everyone at Kalkaringi oval—the ceremony women, and those receiving them—live in poverty. Yet I see again how deep and real their sense of community is.

We drive for many hours. My passengers sleep most of the way. They are exhausted. Yuwani Annie wakes up, and points out a string of flowering yellow bushes by the roadside.

'You can see the yellow flowers? Means fat turtle and all those animals in the sea. Dugong, fish, all fat.' Plentiful—season follows season as it has since the Dreaming. All things interconnected and in balance.

At dusk the convoy stops, and we set up camp at the same railway siding. The vehicles are unloaded, and the fires lit. There is not much wood left on this side of the track. I take my torch and walk back towards the road to follow one of the Tennant Creek vehicles that has set out in search of wood.

'Mimi,' Caroline calls loudly. 'Where are you going?'

'After wood,' I call back.

'With that car?' she shouts.

'Yeah,' I reply.

'Okay then.' She tells me it's a little bit dangerous time

after ceremony. Day and night they keep a gentle, watchful eye on me.

It's our last night in the bush. Annie tells me where to put our tarp. The thirteen of us from Borroloola sleep in a close circle around the fire. The familiar pitch-black sky is the same beautiful dome that has been my ceiling for eight nights. I'm ready to go home too. I can't wait to see John tomorrow, speak to the children.

AS WE SPED FURTHER into the 1990s in Adelaide, the children grew, kept us busy and laughing. Their tastes were diverse and passion-ate. Tim tracked antechinus mice in the national park, played flute and didg with his school jazz band, and animated space-ships. James sang as a bell-like boy soprano, played his Welsh grandfather's violin and scored goals in soccer. Julia dressed up in pink tutus, ran very fast and learned cello. They went to school, scrapped with each other and had happy, uncomplicated child-hoods. John needed nothing more than to see them tucked up safely in their beds every night. Motherhood was the best thing in my life. The way they seized their own lives, in their own way, even then, was a gift.

The business ploughed on too. Wunala Dreaming, our first Qantas aircraft, was so successful that we launched a sister aircraft the following year in November 1995, to commemorate Qantas's seventy-fifth birthday. We called it Nalanji, meaning 'our place', Australia. Turtles and fish tracked paths across blues and turquoises of reef waters. Motifs of coastal camps flashed reds and yellows from a palette of the rainforest canopy. Roy, Barry and Tom from Borroloola came with us on board again, and this time so did Musso. Already suffering advanced renal failure, Musso had had to pull out of taking the trip to launch Wunala. This time Qantas flew his kidney specialist, Dr David Pugsley, with him. Flying over Longreach, Queensland, the birthplace of Qantas, Musso leaned towards the window and watched the landscape drifting by under the plane. Although he'd never flown over this country before, he'd been droving there, and pinpointed the place where they'd buried an Aboriginal stockman in a tree grave, thirty years before, on the muster.

Musso's extra senses didn't surprise me. Going to the Gulf every two or three years in the eighties and nineties was like going through the looking glass. I felt we were living the linguist John Bradley's lyrical description of the Yanyuwa's natural world: 'profoundly full of spirit and meaning, sometimes benign, full of potential danger and indescribable powers'. It was life in another dimension that seemed to me entirely plausible, and there were always stories from another realm that I had no doubt were real. The spirit leaving the body to travel across landscape, the facility to communicate mind to mind, the conversations with the natural and supernatural worlds. The rich spiritual life Aboriginal people had lived for millennia on the Australian continent made all this perfectly believable.

John became afraid of his mental capacity when he was young, shut it out, forced it away. He crashed his car on Brown Mountain near Canberra in the 1970s. His brakes failed exactly as they had in a recurring dream he'd had for years. When we lived in Melbourne before Tim was born, on a borrowed mattress on the floor, I would wake up near the door, John having flung me from the bed, yelling 'It's okay, it's okay!' In that dream he kept having, I'd been thrown from the open back of a utility truck.

He saw the truck in Borroloola when we went back the first time with Tim, and I refused to ride on the tray. The next trip, he said the danger had gone.

Musso told us about the time he was fishing at the mouth of the McArthur. He was close to the riverbank, in the mangroves, looking to spear some fish, when his outboard motor died. Services were thin on the ground in Borroloola, and a broken-down outboard was a frequent occurrence. We would sometimes wait all day by the side of the river for someone to come and pick us up for a boat trip planned for the morning. Spanners and oil cans were always at the ready. This day, Musso said the motor had been working, but suddenly stopped.

A small bird flew down to a branch of the mangrove. Musso said he told that bird, 'You know me. This is my mother country. I look after this country. I need to start my boat now.' He kept trying and trying to start that motor, but nothing. The dark was coming in, and the tide was going out. He was afraid he would be stuck on the mudflat all night. He kept talking, telling the bird who his mother was, his uncle and his grandfather. He told him he always looked after everywhere, sang the songs. He kept telling him 'you know me'. And then that bird was happy. 'He knew me. Knew this was my country. That boat started just when the tide was nearly gone. Just started all of a sudden.'

This sense of 'you know me' happened all the time. We'd go to a quiet fishing spot by the river. Someone would throw some stones, make some noise, call out in language. People were announcing their arrival. Introducing themselves and their connection to country. Paying respect to spirits living there. Some singing would start; songs of the Dreamings in that place. Annie knew after her husband passed away that he stayed nearby in the spirit world.

My husband's shadow always come when I'm sitting like that. And I look back, and nobody here behind, but that's him. I just know. Yeah. Protect me. Guide me through.

There was magic, too. One trip, John's uncle, Roy Hammer, was due back from Robinson River, a settlement a hundred and forty kilometres from Borroloola. We'd been waiting for him the night before so we could get an early start to go out to country. But he hadn't arrived back. When he finally got there, around mid-morning, he told us he'd been chased by Min Min lights. When he was halfway to Borroloola, driving down towards a crossing over a stream, he saw bad lights travelling beside his vehicle. He was very tired, and wanted to pull over and sleep for a couple of hours. But he knew if he did, those lights would kill him. He pleaded with them to leave him alone, explained that he was travelling back to his own country, but they stayed right next to his car. As he sped up over the crossing, his tyre blew. He knew it was too dangerous to stop the car, so he continued all the way to Borroloola on the blown tyre. By the time we saw him, the wheel was just a mangled metal rim. The lights gave up their chase just as Roy entered the Borroloola town limits.

Jemima remembers the magic songs: *Old people been have song to stop the crocodile, used to stay one place in sight. Men sing that song. Old people. For snake too. People been get bite from snake, them old people been have song.*

And Thelma remembers the love songs: *We all got love song, but not singing next to men. Cannot sing near the family, they might go crazy about girl.*

John always says he took a strand of my hair so I could be sung to fall in love with him.

Sometimes we felt the workings of the cosmos during our family trips back to Borroloola. Once, when the boys had grown into young men, we were speeding around the sun-sparkled waters of the Gulf in John's brother Samuel's aluminium dinghy on a hot afternoon. Sam suggested James look out for dugong—maybe he would see one. We did a large arc across the place Sam thought we might catch a glimpse, and a dugong head popped out of the sea. And another, then another. We were surrounded. Maybe twenty dugongs. Sam shook his head and told our James Jawar-rawarral dugong that his brothers had come to see him. Samuel, who crosses this waterway every month of the year to get to his out-station on South West Island, said he had never seen so many dugongs together, and for sure, they had come up to see their brother.

And sometimes the magic followed us. We built a studio in South Australia's windswept Coorong in the mid-1990s. The splendid isolation of this part of Australia features in the film of the Colin Thiele book *Storm Boy*, with its towering dunes, pounding surf and majestic pelicans. The house was on the quiet water side, and looked like a Moorish sandcastle, its two corru-gated living spaces hanging off a rendered wall that followed the line of a seagull wing in flight. On a rocky headland, an almost circular water aspect exposed us to howling gales and the placid calm of brilliant moonlit nights. We'd never see another soul for days on end down there, spending our time collecting cockles from the surf beach and working on collections. One Christmas we'd sailed our small catamaran down the lagoon, the children sprawled languidly across the trapeze of the boat. It was sunny, with a light wind. Scrambling up through the dunes, we came across an exposed human skeleton, probably very old. We left it there, carefully treading our path back in case shifting sands had brought any other bones to the surface. A few minutes into the sail home, the wind whipped up into a frenzy, and the sky covered over with a menacing canopy of purple clouds. As we scuttled down the waterway, a pod of dolphins broke the surface all around us. They were strangely bronze-black, and the local Ngarrindjeri people, who'd lived in the area for generations, said they'd never seen a dolphin in the Coorong.

There were times when sadness took us home—south and north. In September 1994 my father passed away in Tasmania. He'd suffered a stroke during vein surgery. Although he had diabetes and heart disease, his health had been well managed with continuous medical and hospital care. The family had spoken at length with Dad's doctors, and his sudden death from a clot was a shock, but was a risk we'd been alerted to. A few months later, after Christmas, John's mother died too. She'd had only sporadic access to health care in the bush, and the hospital wasn't too clear on what took her away so quickly. Sepsis from her teeth and a heart problem were all the details John could extract from Darwin Hospital staff when he sat by her bed.

My father and John's mother were both in their mid-seventies. My father's funeral brought family together from far and wide, and the deep sadness of the day was tempered by the peaceful placement of his ashes in the wall at the memorial park where he'd wanted to be laid to rest, and where my mother's chosen future place waited securely next to him. Kathleen was buried in the town cemetery in Borroloola, far from the sacred burial site in the islands where she'd wanted her bones returned, as the Law said they should have been.

In our shared grief, the circumstances on every level hammered home again that there was an Australia for my family, and an Australia for John's.

Kathleen and her generation lost the right to their resting place in the islands in March 1978 when the Aboriginal Land

Commissioner at the time, Justice Toohey, brought down a report that he was unable to find there existed traditional Aboriginal owners 'being a local descent group' with primary spiritual responsibility for a number of sites on the islands that made up the Sir Edward Pellew Group. The case was the first claim to vacant Crown land to be made in Australia, heard by an appointed Aboriginal land commissioner under the new *Aboriginal Land Rights (Northern Territory) Act 1976*. The outcome essentially opened up the Yanyuwa's sacred areas, including burial sites, to indiscriminate visitation, development and potential desecration. In every literal and metaphorical sense, it was the nail in the coffin of returning Yanyuwa dead to their spirit homes.

People were confused and disappointed. How could their belonging to this place, that stretched back to the Dreamings of their ancestors, not be recognised? In 1979, they lodged the Warnarrwarnarr-Barranyi (Borroloola No. 2) Land Claim, a repeat claim to have their land returned to them. They argued through their advisers that appropriate Aboriginal people had not been consulted in the first claim, and interpreter services had not been made available to those with limited English. A positive outcome was the resurgence the process inspired in Yanyuwa to document and tell their cultural history—a story that had been suppressed by the galloping pace of social change in the Gulf over all those post-colonial years.

The Northern Territory government did its best to thwart the 1979 re-claim by attempting to gazette a new town of Pellew (the Act precluded claims on land within gazetted town boundaries), auctioning blocks for holiday houses and attempting to make pre-emptive leasing deals with Aboriginal associations (in order to have claimants drop the action). Interest groups were applying their own pressure, particularly Mount Isa Mines, looking for a deep-water port on Centre Island.

But a justice of sorts prevailed, and seventeen years later in Australia's longest running claim to be heard under this Act, land began to be returned to the Yanyuwa. Justice Gray had found in favour of the Yanyuwa, declaring they were the traditional owners of the land claimed, and that the degree of their attachment was very strong. He stated the claimants lived in a manner which maximised elements of traditional Aboriginal life, and maintained their spiritual associations with their traditional country. He recommended that the whole of the land claimed be granted as Aboriginal freehold to the low water mark. It was destructive enough that Justice Toohey had erroneously ruled that the Yanyuwa were not intimately connected to their homelands; the fact that it took almost two decades to repeal the mistake created a crippling hiatus for Yanyuwa culture. Yet again, they were caught in the no-man's-land between their ceremonial world in dispute and the white world casting the judgement.

The federal government has been gradually drip-feeding land back to the Yanyuwa in line with Justice Gray's finding. The most recent, Centre Island, was returned in 2007. After a staggering thirty years, the process is still continuing to acknowledge what Annie describes as theirs from the beginning.

What they doing. Giving back land was ours in the first place.

Annie was a primary informant to the 1979 re-claim.

We very sorry of our country, you know, she said. (If white people come) *they should ask Ngimarringki and Jungkayi. I feel a little bit hurt* (because white people build houses on the island). *Because it's our Dreaming up here. They didn't come and ask, like, Ngimarringki and Jungkayi. We look after country for our Dreaming. Not to destroy it. And for our Business too. Because this is really big country. A big sacred site. When people die and they are in the log coffin, the spirit going back to the place.*

The log coffin was taken to a person's mother's country or their own country, mostly on the islands. The Jungkayi, caretaker on their mother's side, or Ngimarringki, caretaker on their father's side, decided. Sometimes the bones were just wrapped in bark until the ceremony was ready for them to be put in the hollow log. Stones with the patterns of the person's Dreaming were put in the burial place with the log coffin. Those meaningful stones would remain long after the wood and the bones rotted away. Family painted themselves with the designs from the stone for the funeral rituals, sang the songs of that Dreaming, ochred the front and the back of their bodies. If people didn't go back to country when they died, land would get weak. Food might not be plentiful, the sequence of seasons might be interrupted. When people began to be buried at the public cemetery in town, the links the Law demanded to land meant that often just the patterned log coffin would be taken to the burial grounds. Or a burial pole put in country as an effigy representing the dead person. But the ties that had bound people, nature and the spirit world together for thousands of years were suffering untenable stress. Vested interests used the technicalities of white law to appropriate black burial land. Could they have had, in their greed and arrogance, any idea what they were taking?

The connections that survive are a double-edged sword that is difficult to wield. Culture at the centre of life is a vital force in the twilight memories of people born in the bush. For women like Annie, a life lived long in the culture remains her ever-present reality. Yet the passing of her traditions and the face of the future are things that occupy her thoughts as well. She ponders on where the two worlds collide. She sees white disregard for the respect traditional people observed, and a fundamental difference in understanding.

Whitefellas don't understand us, you know. Mmm. That's the way I'm thinkin'. I will explain what things are about, I can talk to them. But sometime I'm thinkin' different.

White men been running around in our country, land. But people never used to running around like that. Aboriginal people. We used to go one way. One way to talk about our place. We got this place. This is our land. And that place belong to somebody else, we don't want to go there. The old people never let people onto land. They died for that sort of thing.

We used to have a canoe, you know. Line for people like me, my father, land and sea, to look for the hunting for the turtle and dugong. And this other line of sea belong to other people. Like the map, you can put on the map.

We having a peaceful time when we alone. Nobody else muck around our land. We can be our own way, in our land. Not other people come, muck 'im up our country. That's the olden day people used to say that.

Greedy no good. Warrki. This greedy can't give to other people. People jealousing for our land. They taking everything for themself. Bad thing. They like something, they want themself. Doesn't give it to other people. They might say, we don't want to give that, they blackfellas. Maybe like that, they say. We don't want to give them good thing. Keep it for our own self. That's what they say. Whitefella mob. I just forget about it then. I feel angry about that.

I really angry if promise not true. People breaking the law, because they telling lies. Too much talk, lies. That's the way white-fellas telling us, but people never talk like that before. White people saying all that, lying people. 'I give you this, and I give you that.' Nothing. You can't get it. He just saying it. If they can't give us anything they talk, we forget it, and we just leave it like that. We cannot make it hard. No. Just leave like that.

Thelma sees two worlds too. And a law of trespass for one, and not for the other. Respect for the ways of one, and not for the other.

European people don't understand. For Aboriginal people, we went to school, and we understand about European people. When tourist come, we know—ah, that's whitefella. They just coming down to do some fishing. So we don't say anything about the land, like hunting them away. So it's good. They want to do that, they can do that anytime. It's important for people, because we have good knowledge from what we went to school. White man school, you know, and we understand people. Like European people.

For us, I think we just thinking about our side. Maybe I think it's good for us to let the people go there, but if we go to the city, and do what we want to do, at the city, you know, make a camp, European people will hunt us away. This is another thing different for us. If people invite us into their place, then we can go, but we can't please ourself to go into their place, European people, but if they invite us, then we can go. If they want us to go, we can go, so we just gonna wait.

Law belong to grandparents. White people, they don't understand. We carry on our Law, too. This how we taught from our family, carry on culture. Our grandparents. How to carry on our own culture. People say we gonna turn into European way, but we can't. We gonna carry on our own Law too. So that is a big respect for us. It doesn't matter we went to school, but still, we gonna carry on our side. You know. The Laws belong to Aboriginal people are very strong. From the grandparents and father. So this what we carry on, telling the people. I think some of the people, like European people, 'Nah, that's rubbish, ladies.' It's not rubbish belong to Aboriginal

179

people. Same we take notice of the European people. When they tell us something about good things, but still we got to look back to our side too. We gotta carry on. Like our grandparents, our fathers, used to get together, have meeting. And then carry on the ceremony.

It is important because this how our people came. Singing the ceremony song, they had lot of different ceremony song. The ceremony song for the death that people used to pass away. And then they used to take the skull into the land that belong to that place, where they belong to that country. So this how all our family gonna carry on.

The determination of Yanyuwa Law women to keep their stories in their hearts and minds, and all the positive things that has meant for their lives and their community, is remarkable in view of them having been subjected to long-term intractable poverty and dependency since the 1960s.

The cattle industry stopped employing people when it collapsed through drought and the introduction of award wages. Few people coming off those stations could go back to their own country, as ceremonial ties were disintegrating from old people leaving the bush permanently, and from workers being dispatched far beyond their tribal boundaries.

The influx of people returning to Borroloola, including those who'd left Malandarri for the town when the bush camp over the river could no longer support the numbers of people 'sitting down' there. Others were returning from the abandoned salt works at Manangoora. The door swung shut behind them all when Malandarri land was subdivided for sale to Europeans and pastoralists took over Manangoora.

While people tried to set up camp in their own groups, tribes were mixed up and crowded together in a way that prevented traditional conflict-resolution practices of conciliation and separation, and white administrators who stepped in to usurp Aboriginal authority extended the reliance that rations had begun.

Governments hurried the process of social disintegration along. Tribal lands were turned into pastoral leases for the benefit of mines and station owners, and the town of Borroloola appropriated land indiscriminately in contravention of the ceremonial complexities and political fragility of this place of many tribes. The growing numbers of tourists decimating tribal hunting grounds added to the picture, and European schools and medical facilities replaced the Aboriginal equivalents.

Together, all these realities had by the 1970s formed a terminal trap that stranded people in limbo. Endemic dependency and poverty were the result. People could go neither forwards nor backwards, as the emerging town of Borroloola had no way nor desire to engage them, resulting in almost total unemployment, while the independence of a bush life had long been abandoned. It fitted a recurring pattern of European colonisation the world over, where the dominant economy wrests control of land from Indigenous people, who then become marginalised within the new society, lose their traditional knowledge, and succumb to destitution through long-term economic and social reliance. Early deaths, chronic illness and substance abuse complete the picture. The Yanyuwa have been a textbook case.

Federal and Northern Territory governments took over from the welfare when the first Department of Aboriginal Affairs was established in 1973. People liked the idea of the change in policy from being directed to making decisions for themselves. But their situation deteriorated, and critics say self-management was three generations too early, that the expectation people could make the transition virtually unaided set them up to fail. Hopes were similarly raised and dashed about returning ownership rights to much of their homelands.

By the late 1990s, we had lost Musso and John's stepfather, Willie. Important leaders. Just a handful of the old people remained, many of them succumbing to kidney failure, diabetes and heart disease. Our trips back to Borroloola always brought the dimensions of the loss into clarity.

It must have weighed on John's mind during those years he was away, that while he was breaking all sorts of moulds in the city, his own family was suffering the dismal legacy of what had created those barriers in the first place. A dazzling soccer career that began as a barefooted urchin on the local oval near St Francis House had seen John become a multi-capped state representative for South Australia, and had led to his selection for Australia and recommendation to play for Arsenal and Everton. As a mature-age student, after years as a fitter and turner, he had matriculated and gained a degree in history and politics, the first Indigenous student with a university qualification in his state. He'd travelled the length and breadth of the country in a beat-up Volkswagen to stir up support for the 1967 Referendum. The highest 'yes' vote ever recorded in an Australian poll, before or since, granted Aboriginal people the vote for the first time. A study trip as a Churchill Fellow revealed to John that the disenfranchisement of Indigenous people all over the world paralleled his own. The fights he fought and won around government board tables were a crusade to right the wrongs that few others at the table could have felt as keenly and as deeply.

The new millennium was looming when we drove with the children to the tip of Arnhem Land on the milky-turquoise Arafura

Sea, camped the red gorges of the Gibb River Road between Western Australia's Broome and Kununurra, and travelled one impossibly hot January to Uluru, suffocating in the swarming heat and flies in Cooper Pedy on the way. It was sobering for our children to see the spectrum of life in their country. Their city privileges of a warm bed, three meals a day and every opportunity from nurturing schools were at stark odds with the poverty that confronted them each trip to the Gulf. The alcohol, the fights, the shanty houses spilling over with kids, Australian kids, who had to grab a mattress anywhere and anyhow they could for the night. And among it all, the pulse of their birthright, a spiritual life that transcended the squalor of Borroloola's material world. Our children's lives have been immeasurably enriched and grounded by their connection to the Aboriginal world.

The 2000s brought the signature design projects we'd been chasing so long. We'd moved the business and the family from Adelaide to Sydney in 1997, admitting we needed to base ourselves amid the scale and pace of the eastern seaboard. To mark the turn of the century, the City of Sydney gave us the CBD's streets to line with Christmas and New Year's Eve banners on an Indigenous theme, a first for an Australian city. Our posters commemorated the opening of the Sydney Olympic Stadium, and our designs cloaked the trucks of a Bank of America cavalcade taking the story of Australia to fifty US cities in the Olympic year. Our whole family roared from the stands with the crowd in the stadium and the rest of Australia when Cathy Freeman carried the nation on her slim shoulders to take the 400 metres gold. Balarinji had been Cathy's first sponsor.

A few months before the Games, on a bitterly cold 28 May 2000, Balarinji art was the official image for the Sydney Harbour Bridge Walk for Reconciliation, when three hundred thousand people turned out to vote with their feet for a national apology to the Stolen Generations. It would take another eight years and a change of Prime Minister to achieve. Our whole family was at Parliament House in Canberra in February 2008 to be with John when he heard it. It was an emotional moment, and he was pleased it was said, but for John, the bigger question of 'what now?' overrode the elation some felt on the day. He wondered what new practical resolve might emerge to mend the broken lives trapped in history's damage. I felt terribly sad for all those people there and tuning in around the country who had suffered the unimaginable pain of such callous separation. The ordinary, humble people who'd been dispossessed of all but the simple joy of family, to see that shattered too. Sorry was a word that had choked in the nation's throat for so long.

Our design quest continued. We presented collections to chinaware makers in Luxembourg, and marketed patchwork in New York. We met with Maoris in New Zealand and with Native Americans at the Smithsonian in Washington and on Mashantucket Pequot lands in Connecticut. The Australian Ballet invited us to create a fantasy tutu for their fortieth birthday; Emu Dreaming's swathes of bronze feathers were dotted with diamante raindrops on classic black tulle, the bodice heavily striped with sequined corroboree body paint. We applied stainless steel patterns to IBM ThinkPads—where ancient and modern technologies met. And we brought the ethos of Wunala Dreaming inside Qantas aircraft; Balarinji's Wirriyarra, 'our home', became, and is currently, the textile for the airline's uniforms in the sky and on the ground. With thousands of staff at Qantas wearing our work and feeling good in it, we feel we are seeing friends almost every day of the week.

Amid our international clients and national projects, another one of those lifetime moments came in November 2006. A friend and colleague, Liz Gibbons at the Art Gallery of New South Wales, had heard that U2's English production designer, Willie Williams, wanted an Indigenous theme for one of the songs for the band's Vertigo tour of Australia. He said they liked to salute the country where they were playing, and this would be completely unique to Australia. A few emails and phone calls to Willie later, and with just days till first night, we worked around the clock with Tim's visual effects studio, Indigraph, to animate a pacy sequence of Balarinji images to backdrop the band. In the sound box in the centre of the arena on opening night in Brisbane, it was a rush to see our colourful graphics, and Indigraph's animation, burst onto the massive screens behind the world's biggest band. But it was something much more to hear the roar of seventy-five thousand Australians screaming when patterns that spoke of *them* and this country lit up the stage to the prophetic U2 anthem 'Walk On'.

And there was a twist. Tim had made a passing remark to Willie Williams the week before the graphics went live. Tim suggested he play didgeridoo with Bono. Willie had smiled wryly, but at 11.30 pm the Sunday before Tuesday's opening he called Tim, and said come to Brisbane with a C sharp didg—Bono wants a rehearsal. A run-through on Monday sealed his spot, and on Tuesday night, as the tour's only guest artist, Tim bounded up on stage for the band's finale—something he would do for all seven Australian shows.

'Please welcome Tim Moriarty,' Bono boomed out to the park. 'His father is a tribal elder from Australia, and his grandfather comes from a little place in Ireland just down the road from *my* house.' The full circle seemed very large and luminous that night.

9

Family

li-malarnngu
My family is the country of my soul.

My family is the song of my life. It leads me across the landscape of my destiny.

Day 9, Saturday 3 June 2006

*i*t's a quick-grab breakfast today. Weet-Bix and some powdered milk. A big tub of tea. Everyone is keen to be on the road.

I take more photos. I'm still not sure if my camera is working. I hope I can capture the faces—refreshed, content from the stillness of the bush and of carrying out the Law.

We drive to the Stuart Highway turn-off. Some of the vehicles farewell us here. They head south to Tennant Creek and Alice Springs. Baba Thelma asks me how much fuel we have. I tell her three-quarters of a tank, plus the spare. She says 'fill 'im up'. Too many nights by the roadside, broken down with no fuel.

We arrive at Daly Waters, the crossroads fuel stop where we will turn onto the road home. We sit on the grassy edge of the petrol station apron, and eat toasted sandwiches. Annie starts to sing a ceremony song. Reluctant to leave it behind.

'Hey!' Thelma Dixon says. 'Too many whitefellas.'

'I don't care,' Annie says.

Everyone laughs. They too are reluctant to stop the songs, the communion. Behind Annie the engine of a bitumen truck is ambling noisily. Two worlds are beginning to merge back together.

Mimi Caroline wanders back over from the roadhouse shop.

'They're all staring at us, those whitefellas,' she says. 'They're rude.' She is upset. Obviously very uncomfortable.

Caroline has a particularly beautiful face. She exudes warmth and grace. I wish it were her beauty they are staring at, but I can see them gawking at black skin and red headbands, at a big group of blackfellas sitting on the ground.

I walk over to buy some drinks. A small boy comes up to me on the steps up to the cafe.

'Will those Aboriginals over there eat me if I go over?'

I smile and ask him why he thinks that.

He points to an elderly man filling up with fuel. Maybe his grandfather. 'He said they would eat me.'

I ask the boy if he would like to meet them.

'No,' he says. 'Too scary.'

'They're my family,' I tell him.

He says, 'You got a charger for my phone?' He pulls a Motorola out of his pocket—I can't tell if it is real or a toy. I ask him what his name is. 'Brandon,' he tells me.

'How old are you?' I ask.

'Seven.'

'Where are you from, Brandon?'

'Busselton.'

I say to Brandon that he is a long way from home.

Half an hour later as we are walking back to the car, Brandon wanders up to Annie.

'Hello, little boy,' she smiles.

'Who's her name?' Brandon asks, pointing at Thelma.

'That's Mrs Douglas,' I tell him. 'Are you going to say hello to Mrs Douglas?'

'Hello, Mrs Douglas.'

There you go Brandon, and your Busselton family. She didn't eat you.

We leave Daly Waters for Heartbreak, and the last stretch

to Borroloola. We pass a pair of sleek golden dingos, one each side of the road, eyeing some young bullocks.

'Husband and wife,' Thelma remarks.

A three-metre *bubunarra*, black-headed python, slides across the track in front of our vehicle. Hundreds of pink and grey galahs fly up in formation from the roadside. A black snake flicks itself up to strike the underbelly of a car coming towards us. We talk about the scorpions that were underneath the ground tarps when the camp was packed up this morning. It is raw country.

By the time we reach Heartbreak at Cape Crawford, there are just four vehicles left in the convoy. Protocols have been observed and groups farewelled along the way. Borroloola is the most remote of the communities. The cars are still stamped with hand prints. We are all still wearing red headbands. The headbands of belonging, of maintaining the Law, of protection from strong Dreamings.

Annie, Dinah and Thelma sing quietly as we drive the last few kilometres of the Carpentaria Highway. I move off the skinny sealed middle part onto red dirt on the side to let the trucks roar past.

Our vehicles wait on the outskirts of the Borroloola township. Windows are wound down, and the women debate where to go first. Annie wants to go straight to the Yanyuwa camp. No-one has been able to ring ahead to let people know the women are coming in. A road grader has cut underground lines south of Heartbreak and the phones to the whole town are out, so they worry that no-one will be ready. But their obligation is to announce their arrival home from the Business. To observe the protocol. Otherwise people in the community might get sick.

We drive first to the football oval. This is where people should be assembled to receive us, as they were at Kalkaringi. But they're not. Instead, an Australian Rules football match is in full swing. Mostly barefooted black kids, as fast as lightning, a smattering of others with boots, and a couple of white players. The fully kitted-up ref is running backwards and forwards, and a small crowd of spectators is scattered under the trees around the ground.

Windows are wound down again, and discussion goes to and fro between the two front cars. Annie doesn't want to stop here.

'They've got no respect for the culture,' she argues. 'They laugh at us.'

'Got to stop here,' Kathakatha Nancy says. 'Otherwise they might get sick.'

The compromise is singing from the cars, windows down. It fulfils the obligation to people at home. Obeying the Rules. A few bystanders glance over to the cars when they hear the singing. The football game goes on uninterrupted.

We drive next to the Yanyuwa camp. Annie looks from the back seat to see if anyone is waiting.

'No-one there?' she says, her intonation rising—half question, half accusation.

We stop the car next to Dinah's house. Annie gets out and sits on the ground, clap sticks at the ready. We all join her on the ground. She starts singing. We clap.

A couple of people emerge from inside Dinah's house, one young woman carrying a baby on her hip. They come up to the women seated on the ground, and hand-shaking begins. Their touch is firm, warm. More come from other houses. A steady stream has started. The singing continues. The men avert their eyes from the women's faces. Old men, young women, young boys and girls, small kids—they all file past to shake hands with the ceremony women who are just back from the Business.

In the centre of the hand-shaking, I see Annie grasp the hand of one of the young men. He has an Eminem T-shirt on. His eyes look away from her. She smiles at him, tears spill down her cheeks, and she resumes hand-shaking. She tells me later, 'They were here. They have respect. They respect the culture.' She is happy. More than a hundred people in the Yanyuwa camp have come to receive the ceremony women home. The DVDs, ghetto blasters and drinking have all been paused while the families acknowledge the culture. For a few moments, this tiny community racked by dispossession and disintegration comes together to acknowledge the power of the Law.

We drive on to the Garrawa camp, where just one household comes to shake hands. A young woman, a young man and their baby. The singing and formalities are carried out regardless, as if they were a thousand.

Satisfied that the Business is finished, that obligations under the Law have been fulfilled, the Borroloola ceremony women disperse, happy to be going home.

I drive back to the takeaway shop on the outskirts of town where John's car was parked a few hours ago on our way in. I'd hoped he might have seen our convoy arriving, and joined us at the Yanyuwa camp. His car is no longer at the shop, and I feel disappointed, a little brittle. I've missed him, and I am starting to feel the weight of two days' driving and an emotional week. The sun is setting and I worry about the hour's drive back out to the McArthur River Mine site to return the car. I am pretty sure I won't be able to change a tyre if one of the spares we put on blows out, and I have no phone reception. I presume John has driven back out there, thinking we've camped another night on the road. He isn't likely to come looking for me if I don't show up. I feel vulnerable, alone.

I drive as fast as is safe in the dusk, but it is dark by the time I reach the mine checkpoint. I am covered in red ochre and red dust. The gatekeeper makes a derogatory remark about the 'dirt' on the car. I start to tell him it's ceremony paint, but decide not to bother. I take a wrong turn after the checkpoint, go back again, and finally find my way to the house where John is staying on the outskirts of the mine compound. It is so good to see John, but I ask him why he didn't wait for me in town. I tell him I am exhausted.

'They said I wasn't allowed to see you there. I had to come back here and wait.'

The women had been looking after me again. Making sure we were protected by observing the Rules. John tells me I look relaxed, happy. I thank him for the connection he has given me to the love of these women. I tell him they are still crying tears for him being taken away all those years ago. He shakes his head and cries too.

'They are so lovely,' he says.

Day 10, Sunday 4 June 2006

*t*he ceremony week is over, and I am thinking about the book. There has been no time to delve into the questions I thought I wanted to ask. I didn't want to disrupt the women's steely focus on the Business. And we were all tired on the way back. The narrow, rough roads meant I had to concentrate. We needed to savour the aftermath of the week, too. Mill it around. Draw from the silence in our heads.

But I do know that without this week, there would have been no book worth writing. It was luck, fate, to be here at ceremony time. To feel the close-knit communion between these women in the Law, to hear their calls of affection across the camp in the early dawn, to share the daily practice of ancient rituals, to listen to the evocative language that interprets their culture.

Annie has agreed to meet down by the river today. To talk about the book, take some more photos. John and I share some lunch on the riverbank with her, and with Thelma, Dinah, Elizabeth, Jemima and Rosie.

Annie apologises. 'I eat slow, Yuwani. No good teeth.'

'It's okay,' I tell her. I cut open an avocado. 'Try this one. It's soft. It's really good for you.'

She likes it. Never tried it before. Elizabeth likes it too. Asks me how to get the seed to grow. I tell her to put some sticks in the sides, and balance it on the top of a glass of water, so the water touches the bottom of the seed. Plant it when the roots grow, and the stem sprouts from the seed.

The women sit in the sun to warm up. I sit in the shade to cool down. John drives away to leave us to our conversation.

I consider which questions to ask. The cultural divide is so wide, the women of so few words, that I am having trouble even framing up the issues. Love, truth, purpose, belonging, compassion . . . the things that endure when any of us peel back the surface. We talk about happiness, sadness, regret and money, and the themes that come back to me are the same.

We look after our families; our greatest happiness is our grandchildren because their parents don't look after them and we have love for them; we don't want any money—we were born without any, we don't have any now, and we will die without any—our sadness is no Dreaming left for our children because they can't listen about the culture.

The children's inability to 'listen about culture', to know the country around them and the country in their minds, will deny them the rules for happy lives. This reality is a sadness in the hearts of these grandmothers.

The astonishing lives of Yanyuwa Law women make the general personal. Perhaps the complicated disaster that is Aboriginal affairs can be less easily dismissed when it comes with names and lives like those of Annie, Thelma, Dinah, Jemima. Although the rest of Australia has never heard them, their voices are clear and strong about a better future. For Thelma, it is a future that has to be focused around the grandchildren, as their sons' and daughters' lives have been decimated by alcohol and hopelessness.

Now today is really changed, you know. Like European people drink, and they don't look for cheek, fighting. But Aboriginal people, they're all for fight. And this why our people gonna fight from European grog, and that's bad thing. So, grog is very bad in the community. We understand they can't look after their children, they can't cook for them, their childrens gonna go to sleep without food. They don't know how to send them to school. So that's bad. Grandparents gonna tell them to go to school, not the parents belong to them. So this is really bad.

Grandparents gonna look after the children, because their fathers and mothers always drinker. And they don't come back to feed them like lunchtime and suppertime. They'll be up at the pub. We keeping them children with the grandparents all the time. We look after them, cook for them, and they have camp with us. They don't want their father and mother to stay with them, because I think grandparents are very important looking after the childrens.

We keep family together, because their parents might leave them, and sometime maybe something might happen to the childrens. Like bad things, killing one another from another man, you know, all the men that can come to their dwelling and they start fighting. And they might hit one of our grandchildren. Well, good family is because we are the mother belong to their father, or mother belong to their mum. So this is very important for every one of us. You can see that every one of us here today, even in other places, we are very important to support our grandchildrens. First thing in our life our grandchildren. When they suffer with their father and mother, we got all our grandchildrens that stay with us.

Jemima agrees. *Because we love our grandchildren, and son and daughter. We love everyone. We got love for them. For other family.*

It is not only nuclear or biological families Jemima refers to. The ties of skin and clan bind the whole community together in its shared journey. In the symbolic relationship to country and in all the threads of ceremony, song and ritual that wrap around belonging.

Learning Aboriginal ways and European ways fits together for Thelma. She wants to see practical changes, too, so people can gain control of their lives.

Well, it make us really happy they go training, another thing they gonna go play football in another community, that is very important for them to go. And we really happy about them learning from other different community.

It is really special for us to go out to bush, like hunting, fishing, and bring some fish back for our grandchildrens, our son and daughter.

We have a building, but sometime we have our family with us too, which they should have their own building. So this is very bad for people, to be crowded in one place. We also have the childrens too. The grandchildren. And that's not enough room. So, we like to see a really good building. Some of us that have one, but some don't. They never get a building yet. Like Annie, she don't have good building. Water was leaking everywhere, past the pipe. This is very bad for people.

We don't have anyone strong like the council to send the childrens up to school, because when we talk to them, they can go halfway and come back, right away down the river. They turn the other way. You know, run away, they don't want to go to school. But we like to see two men take them childrens up to school, that will make things better for a lot of us, you know. We don't want to see our childrens staying in the camp, just mayall, *wild, and the parents belong to them who can read and write and talk proper English. So it's bad for the young childrens. We're trying to have our young men stand strong for the childrens, send them up to the school, so they can get education like us, that is important for people.*

Grog is real bad to community. They buy grog, and they gonna start fight after that. Who is a good fighter. But none of them, you know—they get a hidin' same way. So we really feel sorry about them when they go to the clinic, that is their own fault, they don't look after themself. So women gonna get a bashin' from the men, and that's bad. And the children, they're squealing everywhere, crying for their mothers and father, what they're doing. So this is really bad. And I think it's really bad some man, strong man, don't stand strong and talk in the community about the grog. That we women don't like it. Because we see them childrens astray, starving for food, and we have to feed them, you know. We feel sorry about the childrens. That is very bad.

Annie puts it simply: *See, we just live in the white man's world. I just say it like that.*

Thelma finds young ears in the community are deaf, unwilling to listen to their elders.

We non-drinker that don't like grog-drinker waste money for the childrens, this what we looking to. Take all the government money belong to the childrens, their childrens, and spend the lot in grog. Some people have lot of childrens, they can buy lot of tucker for the childrens. So that is very bad. Using money for childrens, that should be for food, so this what we like to see the parents belong to the childrens, you know. Looking after the money and buy food for the childrens. Lot of food, that can last them till next Friday, or Monday. So I dunno, they too much in grog. So we can't stop them. Because they say, this is my problem. You not right to talk to me. This what people saying.

We can't stop them. What is right and what is wrong. We can't tell them. They always say 'that's our life', 'you got nothing to do to tell us what we gonna do'. So, that's it. I think we like to see the people working down the community, or working somewhere else too, and then, when they get their Centrelink money, they can drink today when they get that money, or only next day, because we like to see them doing a job, instead of drinking grog all the time. This what we like to see. They should help old people, work around the camp, building a bough shade, for young people. The childrens, you know, they can have playground, when they come back from school.

But this is terrible things happening all the time, grog and fight. Bash their wife, send them to hospital. Fighting with other people, they think they can fight better than the other fella, just because the grog. This what happening. They just make themself big. Sometime you tell the person. 'This is my life. This not your life.' This what happening all the time.

Jemima talks about the pub brawls before the hotel was closed down. She says it's better now that they can only get takeaway beer from the shop. I noticed with dismay that the yellow cartons of cans on the convenience store shelves are labelled 'Tribe Pride'. What perverse marketing mind came up with this?

Better now, hotel closed. Big change. When this shop open, they get twelve o'clock, that's it. They get grog till four o'clock, they finish. Then close the shop. Really good. Because when they buy grog here at the shop, when they drink, they don't make noise, and they don't fight. Might be husband and wife fighting, that's all. We sleep really good, no noise. Well they see that pub closed. If that pub open, and if people go up there drinking in the pub, usually people gonna fight again.

But we don't go up along pub. Our kids go there. Boys. Drinking. But we don't go and stay at the pub. But other people there, watching their kids. Boys and girls. And they start fighting. Big mob start fighting, swearing. Terrible.

Despite the temporary closure of the pub, the school principal said 80,000 litres of beer was purchased in Borroloola in the first three months of 2009, with money given away under the Prime Minister's national economic stimulous package. It triggered $80,000 in vandalism to the school. A $150,000 security fence was built to keep the community out.

Jemima sees to the core of the matter. She wants children to be educated, to have the possibility of a job and a future. To heal the hopelessness.

I like see my grandchildren in work, I like see them, my grandchildren go along school every day and learn about white man things, you know. I like see my grandchildren go to university to learn more, so they can help their own people. I telling my grandchildren, go every day along school, so you can learn to read and write. So you know everything, so they can learn white man law, if they go to school every day, and go along high school, and when they finish high school they can go to university. To learn.

So they can answer question for government when they come here. Like meeting with Aboriginal people. Like Amy daughter, she passed away, she's the one used to answer question when white people tell us. We need that kind of people, to learn, to explain the words to old people. So people can understand then. Nothing yet. No young people going to university. Only go along Kormilda College. Anyway, can go university in Darwin, Brisbane or Melbourne. When they finish school, they drink too much. This people here, all the local people, they don't give them job, young people when they finish high school. All the young people go drinking, because no job. They can train all the young people. Maybe builder, or mechanic, all that. Big ones, when they been come back from finish school, that mob should go back somewhere training. Go learn at university. Learn properly, so they can help us.

She worries about so much illness in the community.

Today lot of people get sick. Die early. We only been have flu all the time, along bush. That's all. But this one, when we eat white man tucker, lot of people get different kind of sickness. When people die, that doctor can't tell you, what's wrong your son, you know. Your son been have something, you know, they don't tell us what happened. They don't tell us. You don't know what kind sickness they been have. They don't tell mothers.

Even the doctor don't tell people. He can't tell us what kind of sickness we got in our body. When we go for X-ray, when we come back, that doctor can't tell that person what's wrong. They keep 'em themselves. They don't tell us. Clinic can't tell us. Terrible. Nobody never go to hospital before. We been living long bush tucker. We been have no sore, no sickness.

Jemima would like to go bush more, but it's impossible.

I like living along bush. I like, better for me. Quiet. And happy too. We're happy along bush, because we been learn from little tiny. Our parents been teach us. In town we hear people, drunks all the time. And you can't sit there, noise, too much plane, motor car, tape, drunken people in motor car, running round, up and down. We like stay along bush. Mmm. Just sit down and look kangaroo hopping everywhere along bush. Better to live along bush. But we got nothing to go and stay. We got no car, we got no canoe. We ladies too used to paddle canoe. But this time, nothing, nobody.

Thelma illustrates the breakdown of culture, the broken chain of passing down.

They used to sing us. All the old people, they got that song. Good song. Now nobody got nothing.

Culture is important to us, because this how we got to learn from our old people. And we gonna carry on. We gonna try and teach our young people. They don't, you know, respect us. Respect mean that they don't get together with us. They don't know anything that we singing about. If the European dance, they'll be all up. Like disco. That's the only one they know. But corroboree, public corroboree, if we sing along down the camp, nobody won't come, so we're really sad about this. They don't come near to us. Well, we feel happy about them when they come to us when we have singalong. That's very good for them to learn our way, instead of European way. So they can learn both ways. This what we want them. But in our way, they can carry on and on. Learn from the elders.

Annie knows the old ways are passing now, that she is getting old, and the world for her grandkids is not a good one.

I can't frighten for nobody. Because I'm hard woman myself too, strong. Strong woman all the time since the beginning of my life.

Husband was a good man. He used to help me for anything. We never used to have anything camp, like rubbish. Clean up, my husband. At Wardawadala, we used to stay down there at the station. I still love my husband in my heart. Because he was good for me. Mmm. Hard-working. Making a humpy too, you know, village, for us at Malandarri old camp. And canoe too. That canoe at Sydney, boat now, we made that up the river. That last man made that last boat, canoe, finished then. Big mob used to make 'em canoe. But all been die. This is last my husband now. Last one finished, him. Mmm. Nobody don't know. My husband was a good worker. Really. Mmm.

My life is, I can't do anything now. I just helpless. You know I just wait for my children to do everything for me. Yeah. My grandchildren, Johnny's daughter, and my grandchildren for my daughter's daughter. Carly, Jay Jay, Melita, all them. But I can't name them. Too many of them. They're good kids. Bring my tea and food to the bed. I'm really weak now. I dunno. Sometime I'm good. Sometime no.

All my kids been go to school. Every one. Welfare time, that time. Nobody never used to stay in one place. They used to go school in Darwin. Kormilda College. Grandkids now, nothing. If I make decision for young people, I don't think they'll take it that way. I make my decision, and all the ladies get up, and say, we can do that now. And I am feeling happy in my heart for them. I can make decision for the land, I'm the boss for this land. But I don't know the young people to make decision now.

Thirty years ago, there were two hundred Yanyuwa speakers, now there are fewer than ten. It is difficult to see how the language will survive the passing of these people. In the same way that more than three-quarters of the estimated three hundred Aboriginal languages in use across the country when the British arrived have been lost. As Annie describes, the children have little desire to take on the traditional life. She says even the middle generation, people in their forties and fifties now, have a bush tucker knowledge of their traditional lands—where to find food and hunt. They know only a smattering of the spiritual realm of their Dreaming stories.

If this is a function of inevitable cultural absorption into a dominant society, then the rub is that people have equally been unable to make the leap into the promise of mainstream Australia. They have lost the old, but they have not been able to grasp the new. At the end of the first decade of the twenty-first century, the repercussions of this double exclusion have created a humanitarian crisis of catastrophic proportions on every statistic of parity that might be named. There is no single 'Indigenous community'. There are complexities in negotiating the differences even within the logical split of remote, rural and urban situations. And there are people living functional, successful lives. When averaged out, though, the lowest common denominator is a distressing scene.

Indigenous people in remote Australia die young; on average, seventeen years earlier than other Australians. Men at sixty, women at sixty-eight. The disparity is marginally less pronounced in the cities. The World Health Organization reports it is the widest life-expectancy gap in the world in developed countries with Indigenous populations. Babies are three times more likely to die at birth. People are twice as likely to have a heart attack, and three times more likely to suffer diabetes in their thirties and forties. Indigenous people contract infectious diseases at twelve times the rate of the general Australian community. All this despite eighteen per cent higher per capita spending on Aboriginal patients than others, a slice of the more than $3 billion annual federal Indigenous affairs budget. Inflated, inadequate or misdirected, the funds are not touching the sides.

The alcohol-fuelled violence that Thelma describes is common. A quarter of Australia's Aboriginal population has reported being the victim of physical violence, and one in five Aboriginal people has had a family member in prison— depending on the state or Territory, Aboriginal people are up to twenty times more likely to be incarcerated than their non-Indigenous peers. More than forty per cent of households in remote regions are overcrowded to the point of being a health threat. Of the two- and three-bedroom dwellings throughout the country housing more than ten people, Indigenous families make up eighty per cent of them.

The Indigenous unemployment rate is more than three times that of other Australians, and for those in jobs, Aboriginal households earn forty-five per cent less than the national average. The National Assessment Program in Literacy and Numeracy announced in 2008 that only one in three Indigenous eight-year-olds was meeting standard benchmarks for Australian children. Since this statistic includes the cities, the deficit is undoubtedly more severely apparent in the bush. Illiteracy is widespread among teenagers, and the comparatively few Indigenous students who complete Year 12 rarely attain the necessary marks to enter university, perpetuating intergenerational cycles of social and economic disadvantage. The pleas of Annie, Thelma and Jemima to see things change for their grandchildren are well placed. It is a logical spearhead. And one for which Australia will find a solution increasingly necessary: forty per cent of the Aboriginal population of Australia is under fifteen, proportionately there are twice as many Aboriginal children under four as in the general population, and the Aboriginal birth rate is double the national average.

The 2006 Australian census identified just over five hundred thousand Aboriginal people, two and a half per cent of the national population. Seventy per cent live outside major cities. A high proportion of these five hundred thousand Australians are in crisis. The debate about how to reverse the disadvantage goes around and around the bureaucracies, politicians, advisory and delivery agencies, ecologists, land councils, lawyers, charity workers, churches, businesses and others, as it has for decades. In the bush, it is difficult to find small gains from the situation of embattled communities I visited thirty years ago. Treading water or going backwards is more readily apparent.

Across Australia, Aboriginal people vary in where they are on the trajectory of post-colonial history, and where they are looking for belonging. Some have lost their culture, and don't know their background. Others remember in part, but don't practise their traditions. Dreaming country must be travelled, it cannot be known in abstraction. There is a chasm that Annie's generation believes won't be crossed, between the immersion of their own learning which began before European contact, and the diminishing flow of knowledge to their grandchildren who will find it impossible to connect comprehensively with their stories. These young Australians, caught betwixt and between, have a chillingly bleak future. They are a generation lost, waiting in the wings to join the nation.

Aboriginal people often say identity and land are the cornerstone, the heart of the solutions. But land in itself is a forked road. Should it serve the ideology of repatriation and preservation of rights for what is now disintegrating traditional use? Or is it a pathway to economic participation, with the enormous hurdles of getting the long-term disenfranchised off welfare and ready for jobs or businesses? Australian courts demand proof of ceremonial knowledge and uninterrupted occupation of tribal lands to endorse lineage. As the Yanyuwa can attest, it's a farce that can take decades to play out in the legal system: two hundred years of government-led dispossession has largely rubbed out the evidence. The political lines are blurred between legislative rights and moral rights of social justice for scattered peoples whose spiritual links to land are an historical fact but, increasingly, a fragmented memory. And what of rural and urban Australia, where language and traditional culture vanished, for the most part, long ago? While their lives are different, these people are no less Aboriginal because of their historical fate and blended blood. Far-reaching philosophical questions loom for a maturing Australia if we are to show more compassion in acknowledging Aboriginal circumstance and identity. If we are to try to walk in each other's shoes.

Decency, goodwill and the hunger to build a connection are driving ordinary Australians more than ever before, to reach out and help find the answers. Those who walked bridges at the turn of the century in search of reconciliation, and who cried with black brothers and sisters they had never met in the apology, have an unrequited yearning to cross the line that separates us from conversation.

But how individuals can participate in that intent, and move towards each other, remains elusive. It is a two-way line of access that separates those looking in, and those looking out. The gulf between 'them' and 'us', with its roots in our colonial meeting, when as the Yanyuwa say with such poetic loading and understatement we didn't understand each other, didn't talk each other's language, still carves a deep rift through the nation. There are still painful scars of wrongs to be made right. There are cruel injustices that continue. Governments remain clueless, and spin and political correctness from both sides of the racial fence block the way forward. Alliances shift, and bedfellows of the past may not be partners of the future: the conservation lobby's passion for national parks on the land and on the water is pushing Aboriginal people away from country as surely as the early pastoralists did. Dependency is entrenched, vested interest is rife, and accountability is often lost in excuses. Talk is cheap and words and symbolic gestures, while vital to the effort, will ring true only when we can write a new Australian story that is scripted for John's family as well as for mine.

Pragmatism and empathy in balance might begin to turn the tide. A new educational model in a two-way world would be a powerful start—embrace Indigenous culture in any incarnation that fits the particular family or community, because identity is inseparable from self-esteem. And with equal passion, teach the first world tools to really cut it in mainstream Australia, because if we share equity in a common future there is a chance of equality. Focus with new intensity and expertise on two- and three-year-old children and up. Make the targets ambitious, measure them continuously, build pathways to get the whole country involved and, most important of all, engage every Indigenous person in the journey, as if the nation's life depends on it. Because in history's page, it will.

10

Forgiveness

wunthanbayarra
When I forgive you, I am free.

*Making peace with you cools my head
and calms my spirit.*

*l*ater in 2006, and again in 2007 and 2008, I had coffee with John Bradley to talk about this book. To spend a little time with Yanyuwa and leave again is difficult. Those who come tend to stay or return. John Bradley was in his early twenties when he arrived in Borroloola in 1980 as a primary school teacher. While other staff in the town kept largely to themselves in their free time, John travelled extensively with Yanyuwa families to the islands and along the river systems. His diary and sketches from those trips gradually became the base for more organised research into language, site mapping, hunting and ecological and biological knowledge. In the early 1990s Bradley prepared a Yanyuwa dictionary with fellow linguist Jean Kirton, and was the senior anthropologist with the Northern Land Council for the second, ultimately successful Warnarrwarnarr-Barranyi (Borroloola) land claim.

Because he became fluent in the Yanyuwa language John Bradley was able to ask questions in a Yanyuwa way, and continues to maintain a long-term intimate relationship with Yanyuwa people. His sharp intellect and open heart and mind have enabled him to cast an informed and empathetic light on many aspects of the Yanyuwa world.

I wanted to better understand the spiritual bonds so evident between the women at the ceremony week. I felt those insights might go some way towards explaining the inexplicable: the triumph of mind and spirit among these women in the face of cataclysmic change and deprivation. Despite the breakdown of their culture in their lifetime, it is a powerful legacy they will leave behind.

The way they saw their world was there in the desert, in kin relationships, in unconditional love, in their appreciation for life's smallest gifts. In their forgiveness and acceptance. I began to wonder if only when poverty strips away the rest can the human spirit find its own deep, innate goodness. In the sharing, always sharing, in the constant infectious laughter in the face of material destitution. But it was obviously more, because poverty is as apt to corrupt as it is to empower.

From the ceremony week it was clear the simplicity of their joy of life is distilled many times from the intricate and complex pursuit of the Rules, the Business. From the intellectual and emotional layers of disciplined learning. In the singing, dancing, art, astronomy, parables, symbols and language of forty thousand years of teaching. In the comfort that such a structure wraps around its generations. A vanishing view of the world that I have barely scratched the surface of in twenty-five years of visits to the family. That after just two hundred years of contact, modern society will very soon erase for ever.

The circles of life here are like the layers of an onion. As the surface is peeled back, a balanced, symmetrical view of the whole emerges, ring by ring, in nature's imperfect order. An order that absolves failure and exhales goodness, enshrines truth and emotion. The elixir of happiness flows freely across this most unlikely landscape of hardship and poverty. People deprived of even life's barest necessities exude the warmth of the purest human love.

They are women of few words, the Yanyuwa. But I suspected, after the ceremony week, that much of their spiritual wealth would be reflected in their language. Those sessions with John Bradley confirmed it. So did Annie and Thelma when we sat at a peaceful place downstream on the banks of the McArthur a year after the ceremony week. We talked about a lot of the things that make us human, that offer a commonality regardless of race and place. Like compassion—*ngarramilmila*, which means being brave, showing emotion, having a warm chest. When I show compassion, I'm the one whose chest feels warm. And meaning—*ngalki*, essence, the taste of food, sound of a song, a person's sweat, a skin name. My inner spirit is the substance of my life. On truth—*ihaanjima*— to be straight with yourself, inner beauty. I find beauty when I keep my integrity. About giving—*ngulhu*—understanding your kin obligations, sharing self, generosity of spirit. Being generous is not a special thing. It is just accepting my obligation. And the one we were living at the ceremony week: purpose—*anyngkarrinjarra ki-awarawu*—listening to country, seeing how things really are when the mind is freed up. When the stillness washes over my spirit, then I can see where to go.

These rules for happy lives resonate deep in the language, and in the spiritual dimension where Yanyuwa Law women live their lives. In their decency, humility and tranquility.

We happy because we been happy from the beginning of our life. So we happy, Annie tells me. *Call us* bardi-bardi *now—old lady. They don't call us name, they call us* bardi-bardi. *We feel good, we getting old now. We know what we going to. I know myself we getting old. All right for us, because we getting old. We can't come back to young again. We got knowledge, is important. When we talk, we getting something out of it too.*

Jemima agrees. *We feel good, get old.*

∞

INTO THE LATE 2000s, life felt good for us too, the family and the business 'getting older'. The children had all worked for Balarinji, in various part-time capacities—Tim in design and animation, James in accounts and Julia in public programs. They were proud of their heritage, just as we'd wanted them to be, and had their own dreams of success in the wider world. We'd wanted that too.

Tim Baniyan, at twenty-seven, had added a swag of projects to his company folio, pushing on with building his animation studio. As a child he had drawn endless Star Wars-esque space scenes, replete with multi-jointed robots and orbiting cities. When it came to working up a demo for his first feature film, though, he turned to his own magical stories from Borroloola. James Jawarrawarral, at twenty-five, had worked in jobs in hospitality and computing, and landed a contract as a singer on a ship in Europe. He'd juggled his love of travel with completing an economics degree at Sydney University, and had settled on a career in corporate finance. Julia Marrayalu had broken into the top thirty of Australian women tennis players, and became the first Indigenous player to be world ranked since Evonne Goolagong-Cawley. She'd embarked on an Arts/Law degree by distance from the University of New England while playing professionally all over the globe. We were proud of our children's resilience and work ethic as they pursued their dreams, and equally proud of their kindness of spirit.

John had become an elder statesman for Aboriginal people— for his own community and wider Australia. He'd enjoyed the respect of people from every imaginable walk of life. He'd looked back on a public career spanning forty years, and felt he'd been his own man, his integrity at the centre of every step he'd taken.

I'd devoted a life's work to the design company, and it had taken us on a ride we could never have imagined back in 1983, when we started sketching on the kitchen table, surviving on offerings from the neighbours' vegetable garden. What began as a simple desire to celebrate our children's identity really had found resonance with our aspiration to define the unique essence of Australia. Some of the biggest national and international names had used our work, and we'd been collected by the National Museum of Australia, the National Gallery of Australia, Sydney's Powerhouse Museum, Flinders University Art Museum, and the Centre for Contemporary Graphic Art in Fukushima, Japan. We'd built a marriage, a family and a business, and achieved a measure of security and life choices a world away from the abuse and poverty dished out to John in his uprooted childhood. All our lives have been wrapped up together in this surprising journey we are still travelling.

Then, at the beginning of August 2008, we received an unexpected call from Borroloola. Annie had suddenly passed away. We thought she'd go on and on, treading the paths of mind and landscape the Law had taught her. Then the flu whipped through, maybe she missed the timing of the two-weeks-on, one-week-off doctor, and a lung infection took her. And with her, a well of knowing too deep to imagine. In a community where elderly tribal people are weak and vulnerable, how can a medical service that sends a doctor from Adelaide for two weeks, no doctor the next week and someone from Sydney the week after possibly deliver even a semblance of duty of care? How can it be allowed to happen?

With heavy hearts, we fly into McArthur River on Thursday night. The plane is bigger now, following the mine's open-cut expansion. The culture, though, is the same. The flight attendant holds up miniature bottles of spirits.

'One or two?' to the miners returning to work. Two is indicated by the victory sign. 'One or two Cokes with those?'

The flight attendant chews casually on her return from the galley, her tongue maybe clearing peanut bits, like the ones the rest of us are munching. She is pretty, and the tongue thing is just a little suggestive, just the right amount for the crowd. It's a spanking new aircraft, and it's clear the passengers are well watered and well fed, in the sky and on the ground. It's boom times across the far north, and a man with few ties and simple needs can make a fortune out here. A sprinkling of women too.

As we circle to land, the sky is blood red on the horizon—a burning sunset morphing into black-blue. A glimpse of the floodlights of the mine portside, we bank, then not a light to be seen until our tyres thump the runway.

'As you may have realised,' the attendant grins, 'we have landed at Mac River.' The cold *'a-Mardu'*, as Annie called the south wind, is drifting around. The crisp, soft breeze is a caressing reminder that her spirit will never leave the Gulf. Even if the mine, the town and the tourists who come here are deaf to the power of this old woman's life and the tragedy of her passing. The dimension where she lived her days, and where her spirit has returned, is not easily entered.

We've borrowed a house from Peggy, the baby hidden in a swag from the policeman, and her husband Trevor. The pull back to family after Peggy reconnected with Borroloola was so strong that they eventually returned to live. They've gone to Katherine, a few hours south, to pick up a car, and with their usual thoughtfulness have arranged for a friend, Frank, to collect us from the plane. There are no taxis in Borroloola, and the single rental car that used to be for hire is no longer in operation. Frank drives us the hour into town to Peggy and Trevor's house in the subdivision, 'the Sub', up the hill a little from the Yanyuwa, Garrawa and Marra town camps. Bougainvillea and frangipani straddle wire fences impaled on dusty ground. It is a relief to sink into a swag after a day of travel that began at four thirty this morning. Even with bitumen roads and jet aircraft, it is still a very long way to the Gulf.

I feel sad for our children, that another grandmother has gone. It is another broken link in their increasingly fragile chain to their father's country.

The birds in the morning sing us awake as the sun warms away chilly night air. The funeral will be at the tiny church on the main road into Borroloola. But it is deserted at the designated time of 10 am. A senior man has been delayed in getting in from the islands—boat trouble. Might be an hour or so, the pastor tells us. 'Borroloola time,' he shrugs with a kind smile.

We drive around to the Yanyuwa camp. In the same week, last week, that we heard of Annie's death, we can hardly believe that Roy Hammer passed away too. From lung cancer. In one week, this community has lost its ceremonial leader of the women, and ceremonial leader of the men. I know losing Roy is playing heavily on John's mind. It was just weeks ago we found out he was terminally sick, and suddenly he is gone. A man with a beautiful spirit at the centre of town life. Only in his sixties, Roy adored his grandchildren, and his new young daughter. Taught them to dance like him, Marra way, and to love the sea and the bush. Roy ran the night patrol to cart the drunks away from the Borroloola pub. He loved to share a steak when we stayed there. Eating just a little. Taking the rest back for the kids to have. He'd become a discerning traveller on those trips with us to France and Japan and kept a couple of dog-eared photos in his house. Reminders of a world he glimpsed and liked beyond the Gulf.

And if it is not enough for a generation to be farewelling Annie and Roy, Baba Thelma is heavily sedated in her house in the Yanyuwa camp, close to death, with lines of morphine controlling her pain. Liver cancer and kidney failure are talked of, but people say they've not really been told what's wrong. Last week the *Australian* newspaper reported five deaths in a month in this town, described the grief on grief in Borroloola, asked its readers how many family funerals other Australians might attend in a year, let alone a month.

Thelma is thin, vastly aged, and dozing patiently. William, her husband, is nearby. He cares for her gently. She is drifting quietly away with her family around her. Her grandchildren suck at the breasts of her daughters and daughters-in-law on the ground around a television in the next room. We kiss Thelma's forehead, tell her we love her, tell her we bring the love of our children to her. Her tiny frail frame is a shadow of the savvy, vibrant woman of the ceremony week just two years before, of the years of fishing from the banks of the Wearyan, and of curling up in swags under star-blazed skies. William watches over her protectively.

My mother's death exactly a year before feels raw again. In 2001 Mum left Tasmania—at the age of eighty—to come to live near us in Sydney. When my father died in 1994 she battled the loneliness and fear of being alone in her house for years before she rang one day to say she was coming. Dutiful family holidays and fleeting visits to us on 'the mainland' were replaced by sharing her elderly years. We'd led perfectly amicable but mostly separate lives, and the joy we all found in being together was unexpected. Those years were a gift. Mum became our 'little champion' as she fought and beat cancer, only to succumb shortly after to a sudden illness that quickly closed her body down. Looking so tiny in a hospital bed on the seventh floor of an anonymous city hospital, we kissed her with our goodbyes, her strong, broad fingers touching us for the last time as she smiled through the pain that racked her body, managing to say our names. She humbled us with her quiet acceptance of life and its ending. Breaking our hearts. Teaching us more about living than about dying. I feel close to her spirit here. The rites of passage that ultimately bind us all cut across skin and country and the cards life deals.

Next door to Thelma's, Annie's granddaughter is attaching fabric flowers to the 'hearse'—a white four-wheel drive. Small kids are running around. Family and friends from Darwin, Melbourne, Sydney, Canberra and places in between talk about the community's great loss. Academics from Australian universities who've worked with Annie, the pre-eminent Law woman, are here to pay their respects to her. We talk of the long-time dysfunction of the place, the selling out on health care, and the callous arrogance of bureaucrats, outside and within. We worry for the future: knowledge of culture and Western education, keeping kids at school, continuing the stories. Angst, anger and frustration with so much that is so wrong.

It is midday, and we return to the church. People mill around now. Many of them hold small sprigs of flowers. Some have more elaborate wreaths. Annie's contemporaries, Rosie Noble a-Makandurnamara and Jemima, are by the entrance. They hold us close. John says he's very sorry to Rosie, a close sister to the old lady. No name for her now she's gone. It's the Law. John asks Rosie and Jemima to look after our boys, Julia and me, now his other mother has gone. Rosie hugs us. Whispers so much history, so many stories lost today. That she will look after us. She will miss her sister, the old lady. Just her thumb presses the tears quietly from her eyes. Rosie and Jemima, with their beautiful faces and kind hearts. I'm overwhelmed by their loss.

The small building is overflowing. The wailing begins, the old lady's close family touch her coffin, they rest their foreheads on it. It is important to cry. They loved this woman, who loved them so completely. Her granddaughter is distraught, sobbing, shaking. Her young husband stands behind her, bracing her so she doesn't fall. He cries too. The pile of flowers grows to acknowledge respect. John Bradley gives the eulogy—in English and in Yanyuwa. He is one of the remaining speakers, and it is his dictionaries that may reconnect Yanyuwa people back to their language in the future. He describes the old lady's intellectual clout, her tireless efforts to educate whites in bush ways, and her unerring courage in the face of tumultuous social change in her lifetime. This respected Australian academic is visibly shattered, as his voice builds within the church.

Eighty years ago a woman was born on Vanderlin Island—it is this woman that we come to remember and say goodbye to today. She was born on the north-east coast of Vanderlin Island at a place called Wardi. There is no English name for this place.

This old lady grew up on the islands, travelling by canoe from the islands to Manankurra, Bing Bong, Kangaroo Island and Borroloola. She was a proud saltwater woman, who all through her life carried with her the love of her mother's country and her father's country. She would cry and call out with emotion whenever she saw the white-bellied sea eagle, the Dreaming of her mother, flying through the sky.

She moved through all the country with the old people learning the Law of the land, the names of the country, the Dreamings, the ceremonies, the songlines, and she learned to hunt and to understand her country and the sea. She found her husband at Manankurra, the old man who we also remember today, he fought with boomerangs to keep this old lady as a wife and broke the other old man's arm in doing so. They married and worked on the cattle stations along the coast, Manankurra, Green Bank and Seven Emus, moving along the coastal country where some of her first children were born.

This old lady had little fear of the white man's world, in fact she wanted to know all she could about it. But also she wanted the white world to respect her and her Law and her way of knowing things, and this was how this old lady spent most of her life. There are many white people here today who have been taught by this old lady, she was a generous and hard teacher, the things she taught were important; in exchange it was our job to teach her about the workings of the white man's world, and it was in these conversations that this old lady could really make you laugh.

She was always a worker for her culture and her language and I had the privilege to work with her many, many times and some-times I would say to her, Maybe you are too tired, bardi-bardi, do you want to have a rest? and she would say No, no, I have to put things down for my children, my grandchildren and great-grandchildren, they have to know where they come from. She was the centre of their lives, and they were the centre of hers, and now she has gone.

All of you, what has happened? How did this happen? A few weeks back she was well, she was strong, she was there talking about all kinds of things and walking freely around the camp. Then another story came out. They had taken her into the west to Kath-erine and then to Darwin, and then from there she would not come back from the west alive.

Listen now, all of you! All of you who are my family, I have changed my language, this old lady she was a Yanyuwa speaker, she spoke hard, old-time language, she truly was a woman whose spirit came from the sea. She was a most knowledgeable person in regard to both the sea and the land. She was a strong old lady, she carried with her power of the Law that belonged to her ancestors. She had grown up with the old people, with those who were most knowledgeable and truly she was a very intelligent old lady.

She would sing and dance all kinds of things, matters that were secret and sacred, fun dances for both women and men. She had a good clear voice this old lady. It is so hard to talk of these things. She worked so hard for her children, her maternal grandchildren and her paternal grandchildren, she was always remembering them, she never stopped, she cared for them all and she gave to them many, many stories.

All of you, she has left us all, and we are here crying for her, we are here with tears in our eyes and we feel with intensity her loss, we say goodbye to this old lady, this senior person for all of us, always we will remember her, so now it is goodbye, old lady, goodbye.

Bible readings and hymns flow in and out of the wailing and crying out, common to Aboriginal funerals all over the country. Crying matters. Worth is whether you can cry for people—*jarnararrinji ngililiji*—crying with tears. Amy Friday Bajamalanya calls to the front the old women who lived and worshipped and sang together at Malandarri across the river, when the old lady was young. The place where John was born on the riverbank. A young boy plays guitar to accompany their nostalgic rendition of 'Sweet Bye and Bye'. Some of them take the microphone, telling of their sister, saying they will meet her in Heaven, and calling on the congregation to turn to the Lord and be saved. Not much time, they say, until Jesus comes again 'to pick us all up'. I remember this old lady's words during the ceremony week: *Yeah, we can be Christian too. God give the ceremony to people. Some part of Adam and Eve countrymen were black. We believe in our own way, the Dreamin'.*

We drive slowly in the convoy to the town cemetery. The old

lady's Jungkayis, the men, sit around her coffin in the back of the vehicle. They form a gentle protective circle for her final journey. She'd be smiling at their regard for culture, she'd be proud of what they are doing by the Law.

It is a big turnout at the grave. Perhaps two hundred. The sun beats down as Pastor Vincent, a local man, reads from the Bible. The Malandarri women sing again. The old lady's granddaughter and great-granddaughters sob hysterically and strain to be near the coffin as it is lowered, until Roddy Harvey Bayuma, Musso's widow, back from Darwin for the funeral, tells them, 'Enough now. Come on, get up now.' I hear the old lady's voice from the Law meeting when the news of the death in Darwin came in: *Yes, we are sad, we are very sad. But we have to let it go, let it go, let it go.* For this old lady, there was serenity in death and dying. *We feel good, we getting old now. We know what we going to.*

Alongside the town's children, who know the funeral drill far too well, we scatter clumps of red earth into the grave and say our goodbyes. Only time will truly understand this old lady's passing.

The morning after the funeral, we pile into a troopy with Rachael McDinny and her niece's family to drive out to her sister Nancy's outstation half an hour from town. She lives there with her artist husband, Stewart Hoosan. It's a lovely place on Nancy's mother country. Three houses sit in a scrubby clearing, with solar panels perched on frames behind. A generator waits as back-up. Nancy and Stewart paint their lyrical canvases on a table under a shade cloth stretched overhead, sending them to galleries around Australia and the world.

Hunting is a favourite thing. It is as much the calm of being out there, as the hope of finding tucker. We drive a half-hour from Nancy's outstation, across dirt roads that crisscross the scubby terrain. We pull up under a solitary tree which stands in graphic isolation on the plain. Seven or eight of us fan out and follow the hunters. Nancy wields a crowbar, digging at hopeful signs on the parched, cracked earth of the Dry, where long-neck turtles might be hibernating. Not the best time for hunting, she tells us. November better. Just before the Wet breaks. Still, she got a turtle and a goanna just last week. In the summer rains this place is a full lagoon, teeming with birds, water snakes and small game. It is the place where Nancy and Rachael hunted with their mother and father when they lived out bush. Their sisters too, Isa and Linda.

Nancy suggests we drive further, past Wardawadala on John's mother's country, the place he is Jungkayi for. Nancy chats as we drive in, says it's all right to hunt here, because it's John's land. Tells John he has to go in front, light fire, clear the grass, maintain the rules for hunting on this land. It is both a practical ruse and a cultural rule. Burn the undergrowth and small prey will flee, making them easy targets for the waiting hunters; charge the Jungkayi who has obligations to this country with firing the land to invigorate the aggressive growth that will come with the Wet. Season following season with the surety of the ages. John takes a box of matches, checks the breeze, and lights spot fires in an arc in front of us. The arc soon catches in a blazing ring, and the fire roars forwards. Tree trunks explode with the raging heat. As the flames die down we walk across the crunchy charcoal, stepping over patches that are still burning. Nancy laughs, sits down near a tree, and tells us it's too hot for her feet. She didn't bring shoes. The others dig around in the smoke, tapping for signs of turtles underneath.

Nothing today. And it's time to vote in the Territory elections back in Borroloola, so the hunt is cut short. Bush life and town life. Worlds apart that continue to drift around each other in the currents of accelerating change. We share some bread, tinned beef, and tasteless floury apples. Produce is tired by the time it arrives in the Gulf.

The Thursday after, when we are back in Sydney, we receive the message that Thelma has passed quietly away. The pictures in my mind are of Thelma with our young James on her back looking for goanna; of the peaceful camping place where she and William spread out their swag with us by the river; of her faint, patient smile the week before as she waited calmly for her life to fade gently back to her Dreaming.

Epilogue

IT IS MORE THAN three years since the ceremony week, and as I complete the words for this book I feel sorry for my country for the coming silence, when the songs of the Dreaming will be no longer sung.

There is a vision I have with me every day. It's Annie's soft, grey, billowing hair silhouetted by the flame and smoke of the pre-dawn campfire. I see Caroline's beautiful smile, I hear Dinah's gentle voice, Jemima's wise words and Thelma's knowing laugh. I listen to the beat of women's feet on sand, and feel the deep spiritual strength of their Law. I see the placid face of Rosie, who will take Annie's mantle now she is gone. I think of the hardship of their story, the silent screaming of the injustice of their times, their indomitable courage and their warmth of heart. I hear their pleas to educate their grandchildren, and embrace them in our prosperity.

And I hear, too, the intensity of their ultimate sadness for the coming generation. Who will have no culture, no Business, who won't know the Rules.

They're gonna die, finish without no Business. When we die, what they gonna have then? What will their Dreamin' be?

Annie, what will all our Dreamin' be?

References

Australian Bureau of Statistics, www.abs.gov.au

Australian Human Rights Commission, www.hreoc.gov.au/ Social_Justice/statistics/index.html

Borroloola: Isolated and Interesting 1885-2005 by J.A. Cotton, Alice Springs (self-published)

Bulletin of the World Health Organisation, www.who.int/ bulletin/en

Land is Life: From bush to town – the story of the Yanyuwa people by Richard Baker, Allen & Unwin, Crows Nest, 1999

Li-Anthawirriyarra, People of the Sea: Yanyuwa relations with their maritime environment by John Bradley, PhD thesis, Faculty of Arts, Northern Territory University, Darwin, 1997

Saltwater Fella by John Moriarty, Penguin Books Australia, Ringwood, 2000

Yanyuwa Country: The Yanyuwa people of Borroloola tell the history of their land, translated and illustrated by John Bradley, Greenhouse Publications, Richmond, 1988

Acknowledgements

I am very grateful to the many members of my Borroloola family for their willingness to include me in their lives with love and acceptance. A special heartfelt thanks to the 2006 Kalkaringi ceremony week women from the Gulf who shared their ceremonial world with me and became the catalyst for this book: Dinah Norman Marrngawi, Rose Noble a-Makandurnamara, Jemima Miller Wuwarlu, the McDinny sisters—Isa a-Yubuya, Nancy a-Yukuwalmara, Linda a-Wambadurna, and Rachael a-Mulyurrkulmanya, Maureen Timothy, Edna Pluto a-Maliyawuna, Violet Hammer a-Ringalinya, Thelma Dixon Kuniburinya, Caroline Rory, Topsy Green, Elizabeth Landsen Yayab, Joanne Miller a-Yulamara, and particularly to Annie Isaac Karrakayn and Thelma Douglas Walwalmara who wanted their story to be told and this book to be published. I am humbled by the support and trust Annie and Thelma gave to me.

I owe a great debt to linguist Dr John Bradley, not just on this project, but for the years of willing advice and knowledge he has freely given me. This book draws liberally on his insights and scholarship, and I am grateful for his generosity, particularly in permitting me to include excerpts from his eulogy for Annie. Geographer Dr Richard Baker's work has informed my approach to Yanyuwa contact history, and I acknowledge his leadership and expertise.

Thank you to Balarinji staff Christie Cooper, Tania Occhiuto and Lian Chang for their administrative and creative support, to photographer Marcel Lee for my author photo, and to my friends with busy lives who took the time to soundboard the project and read passages along the way : Margaret Lehmann, Dr Rosita Henry, Dr Janet Penny, Alexandra Sison, Jennifer Dunbar, Dr Jill Sullivan, and Susan Cerato.

I am indebted to my agent, Clare Forster of Curtis Brown, for taking me on as a first time author. Without her belief and encouragement my book would still be a vague intention. I was very fortunate that Clare linked me with an endlessly supportive, skilled and perceptive publisher in Annette Barlow at Allen & Unwin, who together with her team of Alexandra Nahlous, Catherine Milne and consulting editor Ali Lavau, guided my book expertly and with great care. They have made my first book an exhilarating journey.

To my family, I am grateful for your faith in the worth of this book. To my husband John who urged me to write, and whose knowledge and advice guided me throughout the years of working on this project; and to my children, Tim who challenged me to find a personal voice of human story, James for his considered opinions and never failing confidence in the outcome, and Julia who was the first reader and supporter of my manuscript, thank you. You are *li-malarnngu*, the song of my life, and this book is ultimately for you.